Standards in Public Life

*First Report of the Committee on
Standards in Public Life*

Chairman Lord Nolan

Volume 1 : Report

*Presented to Parliament by the Prime Minister
by Command of Her Majesty, May 1995
LONDON : HMSO
£11.80 net.
Cm 2850–I*

Terms of Reference

The Prime Minister announced the setting up of the Committee on Standards in Public Life (the Nolan Committee) in the House of Commons on Tuesday 25 October 1994 with the following terms of reference:

> *"To examine current concerns about standards of conduct of all holders of public office, including arrangements relating to financial and commercial activities, and make recommendations as to any changes in present arrangements which might be required to ensure the highest standards of propriety in public life.*

> *"For these purposes, public life should include Ministers, civil servants and advisers, Members of Parliament and UK Members of the European Parliament, members and senior officers of all non-departmental public bodies and of national health service bodies, non-ministerial office holders, members and other senior officers of other bodies discharging publicly-funded functions, and elected members and senior officers of local authorities." (Hansard 25 October 1994, col 758)*

The Prime Minister made it clear that the remit of the Committee does not extend to investigating individual allegations of misconduct. The Committee on Standards in Public Life has been constituted as a standing body with its members appointed for three years.

Committee Membership

The Rt. Hon. The Lord Nolan
Lord of Appeal in Ordinary (Chairman)

Sir Clifford Boulton GCB

Sir Martin Jacomb

Professor Anthony King

The Rt. Hon. Tom King CH MP

The Rt. Hon. Peter Shore MP

**The Rt. Hon.
The Lord Thomson of Monifieth KT DL**

Sir William Utting CB

Dame Anne Warburton DCVO CMG

Diana Warwick

The Committee is assisted by a small secretariat:

Alan Riddell (*Secretary*), Martin Le Jeune (*Assistant Secretary*), David Jeffrey (*Assistant Secretary*), Andrew Brewster, Vance Duhaney, Steve Pares, Gertrude Bwona, Sue Carr, Jane Mitchell (*to 7 April*), Julie Botley (*from 10 April*), Lucy King (*during oral hearings*), Peter Rose (*Press Secretary*).

Expenditure

The estimated gross expenditure of the Committee to the end of April 1995 is £317,200. This includes staff costs, the cost of printing and distributing (in early December 1994) 5,000 copies of a paper setting out the key issues and questions the Committee would be dealing with in its first report and costs associated with public hearings which were held at Central Hall Westminster from 17 January 1995 to 23 February 1995.

May 1995

Dear Prime Minister,

I enclose the First Report of the Committee on Standards in Public Life. It is unanimous. My colleagues and I commend it to you and to Parliament.

When you set up the Committee you asked us to produce the Report within six months. We could not cover the whole field of public life in this time, and so we decided to concentrate on three of the subjects which appeared to give rise to the greatest public concern, namely issues relating to Members of Parliament, Ministers and Civil Servants, and Executive Quangos and NHS bodies.

Our choice of subjects was vindicated by the public response. We have received nearly 2,000 letters and written submissions, in addition to the evidence given to us by more than 100 witnesses during the six week period of our public hearings. Those who have assisted us with their advice and evidence range from many hundreds of ordinary members of the public to a wide selection of experts, including some of the most distinguished figures in our public life.

They made it plain that the public anxiety which led you to set up the Committee was widely shared and deeply felt. But we found that it was matched on all sides by a resolute determination to see that things are put right.

We have no doubt that this can be done if firm action is put in hand now. The will is there and so are the means. There is no shortage of men and women in this country with the qualities of integrity and altruism upon which our tradition of public service is based. But changes which have occurred over the years in the roles and working environment of politicians and other public servants have led to confusion over what is and what is not acceptable behaviour. This has been accompanied by a number of well-publicised incidents indicating a certain slackness in the observance and enforcement of high standards by those concerned. It has helped to generate a widespread suspicion that much more misconduct occurs than is revealed to the public gaze. Unless corrective measures are promptly taken, there is a danger that anxiety and suspicion will give way to disillusion and growing cynicism.

Our recommendations are therefore designed to maintain, and where necessary restore the standards of conduct in public life which the public are entitled to expect, and to promote a policy of openness which will enable the public to see that their expectations are being met.

Much remains to be done. Such was the quality and quantity of the evidence which we received that even within the limits of the three subjects with which this Report is concerned we have found it necessary to confine ourselves to the main issues and to leave on one side many other interesting questions which have been raised. And of course we have yet to address the other subjects within our terms of reference. We shall start work as soon as possible upon the rest of the task which you have set us.

In addition, we shall, of course, keep the results of our recommendations in this report under constant review, and will return to them as and when the need arises.

We trust that these recommendations will provide a sure foundation upon which we and those to whom we address them can build.

Yours sincerely,

Nolan

Contents

Summary

1.   At the request of the Prime Minister, this Committee has spent six months inquiring into standards in British public life. We have concentrated on Members of Parliament, Ministers and Civil Servants, executive Quangos and NHS bodies.

2.   We cannot say conclusively that standards of behaviour in public life have declined. We can say that conduct in public life is more rigorously scrutinised than it was in the past, that the standards which the public demands remain high, and that the great majority of people in public life meet those high standards. But there are weaknesses in the procedures for maintaining and enforcing those standards. As a result people in public life are not always as clear as they should be about where the boundaries of acceptable conduct lie. This we regard as the principal reason for public disquiet. It calls for urgent remedial action.

3.   Our conclusions are summarised below. They are followed by a full list of recommendations, together with an indication of the timescale in which each should be implemented.

General recommendations

4.   Some of our conclusions have general application across the entire public service:

Principles of public life

5.   The general principles of conduct which underpin public life need to be restated. We have done this. The seven principles of selflessness, integrity, objectivity, accountability, openness, honesty and leadership are set out in full on page 14.

Codes of Conduct

6.   All public bodies should draw up Codes of Conduct incorporating these principles.

Independent Scrutiny

7.   Internal systems for maintaining standards should be supported by independent scrutiny.

Education

8.   More needs to be done to promote and reinforce standards of conduct in public bodies, in particular through guidance and training, including induction training.

Members of Parliament

9.   A fall in public confidence in the financial probity of MPs has coincided with an increase in the number of MPs holding paid consultancies which relate to their Parliamentary role. Some 30% of backbench MPs now hold such consultancies.

10. The House of Commons would be less effective if all MPs were full-time professional politicians, and MPs should not be prevented from having outside employment.

11. It reduces the authority of Parliament if MPs sell their services to firms engaged in lobbying on behalf of clients. This should be banned.

12. Other Parliamentary consultancies and the fact that some MPs have more than one are also a cause for concern. It is impossible to be certain that MPs with such consultancies never allow their financial interests to affect their actions in Parliament, yet this would clearly be improper.

13. Guidance associated with the Register of Members' Interests has led to some confusion among MPs as to what conduct is acceptable. The long-established law of Parliament in this area should be reaffirmed.

14. Full disclosure of consultancy agreements and payments, and of trade union sponsorship agreements and payments, should be introduced immediately. Over the next year Parliament should review the merits of allowing MPs to hold consultancies, taking into account the wider implications of greater restrictions.

15. The Register of Interests should be more informative. The rules on declaring interests, and on avoiding conflicts of interest, should be set out in more detail. A Code of Conduct for MPs should be drawn up. We have set out a draft. The Code should be restated at the start of each new Parliament. More guidance for MPs, including induction sessions, should be available.

16. The public needs to know that the rules of conduct governing MPs' financial interests are being firmly and fairly enforced. There have been calls for these rules to be put into statute law and enforced by the courts. We believe that the House of Commons should continue to be responsible for enforcing its own rules, but that better arrangements are needed.

17. By analogy with the Comptroller and Auditor General, the House should appoint as Parliamentary Commissioner for Standards, a person of independent standing who will take over responsibility for maintaining the Register of Members' Interests; for advice and guidance to MPs on matters of conduct; for advising on the Code of Conduct; and for investigating allegations of misconduct. The Commissioner's conclusions on such matters would be published.

18. When the Commissioner recommends further action, there should be a hearing by a sub-committee of the Committee of Privileges, comprising up to seven senior MPs, normally sitting in public, and able to recommend penalties when appropriate. MPs who are being heard should be entitled to be accompanied by advisers.

Ministers and Civil Servants

19. Very high standards of conduct are rightly expected from Ministers and civil servants. While there is public disquiet, this focuses on fairly narrow issues.

20. A Code of Conduct for civil servants has recently been announced. The existing guidance for Ministers is sound but needs to be drawn together into a clear set of principles.

21. The public interest requires that allegations of Ministerial misconduct should be promptly investigated. Normally this is a matter for the Prime Minister. Who should investigate, and whether to publish a report, will vary from case to case, but in such cases civil servants should not be drawn into the party debate and their advice should remain confidential.

22. There has been much concern over Ministers who, on leaving office, take positions in companies with which they have had official dealings. For two years after leaving office senior civil servants have to seek clearance from an independent advisory committee before joining private companies. The same need to protect the public interest arises with Ministers and special advisers, who should be subject to a similar clearance system.

23. For both Ministers and civil servants the system should be made more open to public scrutiny than at present.

24. There is insufficient monitoring of the effectiveness of similar arrangements for more junior civil servants, and these should be reviewed.

25. Very large changes in the management and structure of the civil service have taken place. Greater delegation and diversity mean that more positive action has to be taken to reduce the risk of impropriety. In particular, political interference in the pay and promotion of individuals must be avoided.

26. While the new independent appeal system for civil servants is welcome, better arrangements within departments for the confidential investigation of staff concerns on propriety are needed.

27. More needs to be done to ensure that all civil servants remain aware of the standards of conduct required in the public sector.

28. The rules on acceptance of gifts and hospitality for both Ministers and civil servants are sufficiently strict, and need not be changed.

Quangos (Executive NDPBs and NHS bodies)

29. Executive Non-Departmental Public Bodies (NDPBs) and National Health Service bodies are public bodies with executive powers whose Boards are appointed by Ministers. They have almost 9000 Board Members and spend some £40bn a year.

30. There is much public concern about appointments to Quango Boards, and a widespread belief that these are not always made on merit. The Government has committed itself publicly to making all appointments on merit.

31. While individual posts should always be filled purely on merit, it is important that the overall composition of boards should represent an appropriate mix of relevant skills and background. This range should be clearly and publicly set out in job specifications.

32. Ministers should continue to make board appointments, but an independent Public Appointments Commissioner should be appointed to regulate, monitor and report on the public appointments process.

33. The government is already taking steps to develop best practice and to ensure that the widest range of candidates is secured. In future the Commissioner should recommend best practice and departments should have to justify any departures from it.

34. Formal and impartial assessment of candidates is essential. The advisory panels being introduced in the NHS should become universal, and they should all include an independent element. All candidates whom Ministers consider for all appointments should have been approved as suitable by an advisory panel.

35. Following recent scandals, much has been done to improve and standardise arrangements to secure high standards of conduct in NDPBs. This process needs to continue. All NDPBs and NHS bodies should have codes of conduct, in line with the principles which apply to all public bodies, for board members and staff.

36. There remain differences in the legal framework governing standards of conduct in NDPBs, NHS bodies and local authorities. The government needs to review this area and consider whether greater consistency can be achieved.

37. Further steps are needed to safeguard propriety both internally and externally. Internally, the Accounting Officer's responsibility for propriety as well as financial matters needs to be emphasised, and better confidential avenues are needed for investigation of staff concerns about propriety.

38. Externally, the role of auditors in propriety matters needs to be emphasised. Audit arrangements should be reviewed to ensure that best practice applies to all bodies.

List of Recommendations

We set out below our specific recommendations under each of the main headings of our report (followed in brackets by the paragraph number within the chapter).

We believe it would be helpful to those to whom we have addressed the Report if we gave some broad indication of the timescale within which we consider that recommendations could be implemented. We therefore place our recommendations into one of three broad categories:

A   **those recommendations which we believe could be implemented with the minimum of delay;**

B   **those recommendations which could in our view be implemented—or on which we would expect to see significant progress towards implementation—by the end of this year;**

C   **recommendations which we recognise will take longer to implement, but on which we would wish to re-examine progress in the latter part of next year.**

Members of Parliament

1.   Members of Parliament should remain free to have paid employment unrelated to their role as MPs.   (para 2.21) A

2.   The House of Commons should restate the 1947 resolution which places an absolute bar on Members entering into contracts or agreements which in any way restrict their freedom to act and speak as they wish, or which require them to act in Parliament as representatives of outside bodies.   (para 2.59) A

3.   The House should prohibit Members from entering into any agreements in connection with their role as Parliamentarians to undertake services for or on behalf of organisations which provide paid Parliamentary services to multiple clients or from maintaining any direct or active connections with firms, or parts of larger firms, which provide such Parliamentary services.   (para 2.59) B

4.   The House should set in hand without delay a broader consideration of the merits of Parliamentary consultancies generally, taking account of the financial and political funding implications of change.   (para 2.59) A

5.   The House should:

- require agreements and remuneration relating to Parliamentary services to be disclosed;

- expand the guidance on avoiding conflicts of interest;

- introduce a new Code of Conduct for Members;

- appoint a Parliamentary Commissioner for Standards;

- establish a new procedure for investigating and adjudicating on complaints in this area about Members.   (para 2.59) B

6.   On disclosure of interests we recommend:

- the Register should continue broadly in its present form, and should be published annually. However the detailed entry requirements should be improved to give a clearer description of the nature and scope of the interests declared;

- updating of the Register should be immediate. The current updated version should be made more widely available electronically;

- from the beginning of the 1995/96 session (expected in November) Members should be required to deposit in full with the Register any contracts relating to the provision of services in their capacity as Members, and such contracts should be available for public inspection;

- from the same time, Members should be required to declare in the Register their annual remuneration, or estimated annual remuneration, in respect of such agreements. It would be acceptable if this were done in bands: eg under £1,000; £1,000–5,000; £5,000–10,000; then in £5,000 bands. An estimate of the monetary value of benefits in kind, including support services, should also be made;

- Members should be reminded more frequently of their obligations to Register and disclose interests, and that Registration does not remove the need for declaration and better guidance should be given, especially on first arrival in the House.   (para 2.70) B

7.   Members should be advised in their own interests that all employment agreements which do not have to be deposited should contain terms, or be supported by an exchange of letters, which make it clear that no activities relating to Parliament are involved.

(para 2.71) B

8.   The rules and guidance on avoiding conflict of interest should be expanded to cover the whole range of business pertaining to Parliament, and particular attention should be paid to Standing Committees.   (para 2.85) B

9. The House should draw up a Code of Conduct setting out the broad principles which should guide the conduct of Members; this should be restated in every new Parliament.

(para 2.89) B

10. The Government should now take steps to clarify the law relating to the bribery of or the receipt of a bribe by a Member of Parliament. (para 2.104) C

11. On procedure we recommend:

- the House should appoint a person of independent standing, who should have a degree of tenure and not be a career member of the House of Commons staff, as Parliamentary Commissioner for Standards;

- the Commissioner should have the same ability to make findings and conclusions public as is enjoyed by the Comptroller and Auditor General and the Parliamentary Commissioner for Administration;

- the Commissioner should have independent discretion to decide whether or not a complaint merits investigation or to initiate an investigation;

- the Commissioner should be able to send for persons, papers and records, and will therefore need to be supported by the authority of a Select Committee with the necessary powers;

- we consider that a sub-committee of the Committee of Privileges, consisting of up to seven very senior Members, would be the best body to take forward individual cases recommended by the Commissioner for further consideration; we recommend that such a sub-committee should be established;

- in view of the fact that there would be a prima facie case to investigate, we recommend that hearings of the proposed sub-committee should normally be in public. We also recommend that the sub-committee should be able to call on the assistance of specialist advisers and that a Member who so wishes should be able to be accompanied by advisers before the sub-committee;

- the sub-committee should be given discretion to enable an adviser to act as the Member's representative at hearings;

- as the sub-committee would report to the full Privileges Committee this would have the practical effect of giving the Member a right of appeal to that Committee. Only the most serious cases should need to be considered by the whole House. (2.104) B

The Executive: Ministers and Civil Servants

12. The first paragraph of Questions of Procedure for Ministers (QPM) should be amended to say: 'It will be for individual Ministers to judge how best to act in order to uphold the highest standards. It will be for the Prime Minister to determine whether or not they have done so in any particular circumstance.' (para 3.13) A

13. The Prime Minister should put in hand the production of a document drawing out from QPM the ethical principles and rules which it contains to form a free-standing code of conduct or a separate section within a new QPM. If QPM is to remain the home for this guidance, we recommend that it is retitled 'Conduct and Procedure for Ministers' to reflect its scope. (para 3.15) A/B

14. Careful consideration should be given to ensuring that the most appropriate means is used for the investigation of cases of alleged impropriety affecting Ministers. Other than in exceptional circumstances, the general rule that advice from civil servants to Ministers should not be made public should apply in these cases. (para 3.22) A

15. A system similar to the civil service business appointment rules should apply to Ministers. The system should operate on an advisory basis, and it should be administered by the existing Advisory Committee on Business Appointments. (para 3.31) A

16. In parallel with the civil service arrangements for permanent secretaries, an automatic waiting period of three months should apply to former Cabinet Ministers, but not to other Ministers or Whips. In cases where a further waiting period is recommended, the maximum waiting period should be set at two years from the date of leaving office. (para 3.33) A

17. The advisory committee should be able to advise an applicant, whether a civil servant or a former Minister, that they feel that the application is not appropriate, and to make public that advice if it is not taken. (para 3.34) A

18. Former Ministers, having received the advice of the advisory committee, should have the right of appeal to the Prime Minister of the day, who would be able to reduce any waiting period or relax any conditions if the appeal were well-founded. (para 3.36) A

19. The system should be as open as possible, while protecting the personal privacy of Ministers. (para 3.38) A

20. The Government should monitor the workload of the advisory committee under the new arrangements and put in place contingency arrangements for its staffing to be augmented to deal with the aftermath of any change of administration. (para 3.39) B

21. Departments, as well as maintaining records of gifts, should maintain records of hospitality accepted by Ministers in their official capacity and should make these records available if asked to do so. (para 3.41) A

22. The new performance pay arrangements for the senior civil service should be structured so as not to undermine political impartiality. (para 3.48) A

23. The draft civil service code should be revised to cover circumstances in which a civil servant, while not personally involved, is aware of wrongdoing or maladministration taking place. (para 3.51) A

24. The operation of the appeals system under the Code should be disseminated as openly as possible, and the Commissioners should report all successful appeals to Parliament. (para 3.52) B

25. Departments and agencies should nominate one or more officials entrusted with the duty of investigating staff concerns raised confidentially. (para 3.53) A

26. The new civil service code should be introduced with immediate effect, without waiting for legislation. (para 3.55) A

27. The Cabinet Office should continue to survey and disseminate best practice on maintaining standards of conduct to ensure that basic principles of conduct are being properly observed. (para 3.59) A

28. There should be regular surveys in departments and agencies of the knowledge and understanding staff have of ethical standards which apply to them; where such surveys indicate problem areas, guidance should be reinforced and disseminated appropriately, particularly by way of additional training. (para 3.61) A

29. The Advisory Committee on Business Appointments should, when an appointment has been taken up, give the reasons for its decision in that particular case. (para 3.66) A

30. The operation, observance and objectives of the civil service business appointment rules should be reviewed. (para 3.68) B

31. Special advisers should be subject to the business appointment rules. (para 3.70) A

32. A central or local record of invitations and offers of hospitality accepted should be kept in all departments and agencies. There should be clear rules specifying the circumstances in which staff should seek management advice about the advisability of accepting invitations and offers of hospitality. (para 3.72) A

Quangos
(Executive Non-Departmental Public bodies and National Health Service Bodies)

Appointments

33. The ultimate responsibility for appointments should remain with Ministers. (para 4.29) A

34. All public appointments should be governed by the overriding principle of appointment on merit. (para 4.35) A

35. Selection on merit should take account of the need to appoint boards which include a balance of skills and backgrounds. The basis on which members are appointed and how they are expected to fulfil their role should be explicit. The range of skills and background which are sought should be clearly specified.   (para 4.46) A

36. All appointments to executive NDPBs or NHS bodies should be made after advice from a panel or committee which includes an independent element.   (para 4.48) C

37. Each panel or committee should have at least one independent member and independent members should normally account for at least a third of membership.
                                                                                          (para 4.49) C

38. A new independent Commissioner for Public Appointments should be appointed, who may be one of the Civil Service Commissioners.   (para 4.53) B

39. The Public Appointments Commissioner should monitor, regulate and approve departmental appointments procedures.   (para 4.55) C

40. The Public Appointments Commissioner should publish an annual report on the operation of the public appointments system.   (para 4.56) C

41. The Public Appointments Unit should be taken out of the Cabinet Office and placed under the control of the Public Appointments Commissioner.   (para 4.57) B

42. All Secretaries of State should report annually on the public appointments made by their departments.   (para 4.62) B

43. Candidates for appointment should be required to declare any significant political activity (including office-holding, public speaking and candidature for election) which they have undertaken in the last five years.   (para 4.68) B

44. The Public Appointments Commissioner should draw up a code of practice for public appointments procedures. Reasons for departures from the code on grounds of "proportionality" should be documented and capable of review.   (para 4.72) C

Propriety

45. A review should be undertaken by the Government with a view to producing a more consistent legal framework governing propriety and accountability in public bodies, including executive NDPBs, NHS bodies and local government. This should involve all relevant departments and be co-ordinated by the Cabinet Office and the Treasury.
                                                                                          (para 4.81) C

46. The adoption of a code of conduct for board members should be made mandatory for each executive NDPB and NHS body.   (para 4.91) B

47. It should be mandatory for the board of each executive NDPB and NHS body to adopt a code of conduct for their staff.   (para 4.91) B

48. Board members and staff of all executive NDPBs and NHS bodies should be required on appointment to undertake to uphold and abide by the relevant code, and compliance should be a condition of appointment. (para 4.95) B

49. Sponsor departments should develop clear disciplinary procedures for board members of executive NDPBs and NHS bodies with appropriate penalties for failing to observe codes of conduct. (para 4.96) C

50. The role of executive NDPB and NHS accounting officers should be redefined to emphasise their formal responsibility for all aspects of propriety. (para 4.102) B

51. The Audit Commission should be authorised to publish public interest reports on NHS bodies at its own discretion. (para 4.105) B

52. The Treasury should review the arrangements for external audit of public bodies, with a view to applying the best practices to all. (para 4.109) C

53. Each Executive NDPB and NHS body that has not already done so should nominate an official or Board Member entrusted with the duty of investigating staff concerns about propriety raised confidentially. Staff should be able to make complaints without going through the normal management structure, and should be guaranteed anonymity. If they remain unsatisfied, staff should also have a clear route for raising concerns about issues of propriety with the sponsor department. (para 4.116) B

54. Executive NDPBs, supported by their sponsor departments, should:

- develop their own codes of openness, building on the government code and developing good practice on the lines recommended in this report;

- ensure that the public are aware of the provisions of their codes;

sponsor departments should:

- encourage executive bodies to follow best practice and improve consistency between similar bodies by working to bring the standards of all up to those of the best;

the Cabinet Office should:

- produce and periodically update guidance on good practice for openness in executive NDPBs and NHS bodies. (para 4.123) B

55. New board members should on appointment make a commitment to undertake induction training which should include awareness of public sector values, and standards of probity and accountability. (para 4.125) B

The Seven Principles of Public Life

Selflessness
Holders of public office should take decisions solely in terms of
the public interest. They should not do so in order to gain
financial or other material benefits for themselves,
their family, or their friends.

Integrity
Holders of public office should not place themselves under any
financial or other obligation to outside individuals or organisations
that might influence them in the performance
of their official duties.

Objectivity
In carrying out public business, including making public
appointments, awarding contracts, or recommending individuals
for rewards and benefits, holders of public office
should make choices on merit.

Accountability
Holders of public office are accountable for their decisions and actions to
the public and must submit themselves to whatever scrutiny is
appropriate to their office.

Openness
Holders of public office should be as open as possible about all
the decisions and actions that they take. They should give reasons for
their decisions and restrict information only when the
wider public interest clearly demands.

Honesty
Holders of public office have a duty to declare any private interests
relating to their public duties and to take steps to resolve any conflicts
arising in a way that protects the public interest.

Leadership
Holders of public office should promote and support these
principles by leadership and example.

• •

These principles apply to all aspects of public life.
The Committee has set them out here for the benefit of
all who serve the public in any way.

Chapter 1

Introduction

1. In October 1994 the Prime Minister asked this Committee to enquire into the growing public concern about standards in public life. Evidence of such concern was reflected in the correspondence which we received nearly 2,000 letters of all kinds from people in every walk of life. It was also voiced by many of the 100 witnesses who gave evidence to us in public over a period of six weeks. Further indications of widespread public concern over the trustworthiness of politicians were contained in recent opinion surveys, details of which are set out in Appendix 1 to this report.

2. It was equally clear from a considerable body of this evidence that much of the public anxiety about standards of conduct in public life is based upon perceptions and beliefs which are not supported by the facts. Taking the evidence as a whole, we believe that the great majority of men and women in British public life are honest and hard working, and observe high ethical standards.

3. There is, and always will be, a minority who fall short. Deliberate corruption is, however, notoriously difficult to measure. As our predecessors on the Salmon Commission wrote, 'there is no objective way of making a true assessment of the amount of public sector corruption that exists now or whether the amount has changed over recent decades.'*

4. It is equally difficult to say whether there has been any decline in overall standards in public life. The public's concerns about the conduct of people in public life certainly seem to have increased in recent years, but part of the explanation may be that the public's expectations of the behaviour of those in office are now higher[†]. The amount of media interest in the subject of misconduct in public life, particularly sexual misconduct, has certainly intensified. Politicians of previous generations, and their families, were largely free from the invasions of privacy by the press which are now common. In recent years there have been periods when instances of real or alleged malpractice seemed to be reported in the newspapers every few weeks. There is no precedent in this century for so many allegations of wrongdoing, on so many different subjects, in so short a period of time. It is not therefore surprising that opinion polls suggest that people believe that there is more actual misconduct than in the past.

5. It would be comforting to think that the public believe that standards have declined only because of the growth in media activity and intrusion into the private lives of public figures. Yet we do not believe that this is the whole answer. The newspapers may have run

---

*   Report of the Royal Commission on Standards of Conduct in Public Life, Cmnd 6524, 1976, paragraph 34.

†   A brief look at the historical background to our work is contained appendix 1.

with or encouraged the 'sleaze' issue, but they generally print what they believe to be the facts and can be challenged in court if what they say is defamatory or untrue. A free press using fair techniques of investigative journalism is an indispensable asset to our democracy. We would prefer more acknowledgement from the media that the overwhelming majority of public servants work hard and have high standards. We would prefer more recognition of the value of our democratic mechanisms and the dangers of undermining them. We would prefer less concentration on private sexual behaviour. But we do not hold the media in any way to blame for exposing genuine wrongdoing. They have a duty to enquire— coupled with a duty to do so responsibly—and in that way can contribute to the preservation of standards in public life.

> *"... We are in a period which I think is nothing like as bad as the Edwardian and early Georgian period but is, nonetheless, one that does give rise to a good deal of unease."* **Lord Blake (witness)**
>
> *"The principles of honesty, truth and integrity have become debased at the highest levels of society, by people who should be in their personal and private lives examples to ordinary people."* **Mavis Evans (correspondent)**
>
> *"The standard of public behaviour of politicians in this country does compare well with many comparable countries."* **Ivor Crewe (witness)**
>
> *"Most people who join the House of Commons as Members are as animated with the idea of public service as they were 50 years ago."* **Lord Callaghan (witness)**
>
> *"As a parent of two teenagers and a schoolteacher of pupils aged 11–16 years, I am deeply disappointed that public figures appear to escape retribution for actions and attitudes which set such a poor example to our youth."* **David Powell (correspondent)**

6.   Frequently in our work we heard the expression 'grey area' used as a rationalisation of morally dubious behaviour. The ubiquity of the phrase, and the implication that some no longer seem to be certain of the difference between what is right and what is wrong in public life, concern us. When people in public life are in doubt about whether a particular action is consistent with the standards expected of them, the only proper course is not to do it.

7.   The erosion of public confidence in the holders of public office is a serious matter. One of our aims in this report is to rebuild this public confidence. The other is to try to restore some clarity and direction wherever moral uncertainty has crept in. In so far as a culture of moral vagueness, a 'culture of sleaze', has developed, we seek to put an end to it. A degree of austerity, of respect for the traditions of upright behaviour in British public life, is not only desirable, but essential.

8.   We recommend procedures and institutions that will deter and detect wrong-doing. We seek to restore respect for the ethical values inherent in the idea of public service. Formal procedures have a role to play, but in the end it is individuals' consciences that matter.

9.   There are two reasons why this is important. First, we in Britain have, with reason, always prided ourselves on the standards of conduct of the vast majority of our public servants; that pride must be restored. Second, experience elsewhere warns that, unless the strictest standards are maintained and where necessary restored, corruption and malpractice can become part of the way of life. The threat at the moment is not great. Action needs to be taken before it becomes so.

10.   Changes in the public sector have increased the need to take action. Decentralisation and contracting out have varied the format for organisations giving public service. There is greater interchange between sectors. There are more short term contracts. There is scepticism about traditional institutions. Against that background, it cannot be assumed that everyone in the public service will assimilate a public service culture unless they are told what is expected of them and the message is systematically reinforced. The principles inherent in the ethic of public service need to be set out afresh. We have done so on page 14.

11.   To consider what lessons might be learned from experience overseas, we have obtained information (both written and in talks with knowledgeable visitors) about arrangements existing or under consideration in a number of other European Union and Commonwealth countries and the United States. We found closer analogies where the constitutional framework was based on the Westminster model. While we noted a tendency in recent years to underpin rules of conduct with statute law, we also noted a current of opinion in Canada and elsewhere that there are advantages in having a more flexible non-statutory basis for Codes of Conduct. We concluded that it was appropriate to United Kingdom circumstances to tailor our recommendations closely to our largely non-statutory mechanisms.

12.   Our remit covers the whole of public life. In order to make our task more manageable, we decided to concentrate in this first report on three of the areas which seemed to cause most immediate public concern: the House of Commons, central Government (Ministers and civil servants) and executive quangos, including NHS bodies. These represent a broad swathe of public life, and they are covered in the next three chapters of our report. We believe that the seven principles set out on page 14 are applicable to them all, and to those parts of public life we will cover later.

Common threads

13.   We have also given thought to the mechanisms which need to be put in place to ensure that our principles are understood.

Codes of Conduct

14.   We believe that the principles set out above should form the basis of codes of conduct throughout the public sector. Ministers have recently accepted a new code for the civil service. Most of the quangos mentioned in this report already have codes. Later in this report we comment on these and also recommend codes for Ministers and Members of Parliament.

15. Such codes should be drawn up within each organisation concerned, so that they will be appropriate to their circumstances and will form part of the culture of the organisation. But they should all be based on the principles set out above. In addition to the principles and the codes two other common elements will be found throughout this report.

Independent Scrutiny

16. First, wherever there is scope for behaviour falling below the highest standards, then internal systems must be supported by independent scrutiny and monitoring. Part of this will be routinely performed by auditors, but in certain circumstances an independent body to oversee the framework within which actions are taken and to monitor compliance can be an important additional safeguard in maintaining public confidence.

Guidance and Education

17. Second, because of the pace of change, it is essential that more is done to inculcate high ethical standards through guidance, education, and training, particularly induction training, than has been thought necessary in the past. In this context guidance means the planned promotion and reinforcement throughout every public body of ethical standards. It involves the active participation of people in public life in formulating key ethical standards; it requires those in senior positions to set a good example; and it requires organisations to monitor the awareness of those standards and take remedial action when necessary.

Conclusion

18. We have inherited a legacy of immense value from those who laid the foundations of a public service in the last century and in this that people could trust and in which they could take pride. As Robert Sheldon MP, the Chairman of the Public Accounts Committee, told us:

> *'We are extraordinarily fortunate—there are, what, 184 countries in the United Nations. The number of them which have standards somewhere approaching ours are just a handful. We are a rare exception and it is up to us to make sure that we retain those standards... Once you lose them I am afraid it is extraordinarily difficult to return to them'.*

19. The recommendations we make in this report are designed to ensure that public life in Britain retains the highest standards.

Chapter 2

Members of Parliament

Principal Conclusions

Members of Parliament should remain free to have paid outside interests unrelated to the work of Parliament. Paid work as general multi-client Parliamentary consultants should be banned. The House of Commons should review the law of Parliament with regard to other Parliamentary consultancies. We will review the situation further in a year's time.

Agreements and remuneration in respect of permitted Parliamentary consultancies and sponsorships should be declared in full. Other entries in the Register of Members' Interests should more clearly identify the nature of the interest.

The 1947 Resolution of the House on paid outside interests should be reaffirmed. Clearer and more detailed guidance should be issued on declarations of interest, and on action to avoid conflicts of interest.

A Code of Conduct for Members of Parliament should be drawn up.

The House should appoint a person of independent standing as Parliamentary Commissioner for Standards, who would maintain the Register of Interests, advise on the Code of Conduct, provide guidance and advice on matters of conduct and interests, and investigate and report on complaints about Members' conduct.

When the Commissioner has found in a matter of conduct that a Member has a case to answer, this should be heard by a sub-committee of the Committee of Privileges under arrangements which would combine the rules of natural justice more effectively with the established procedures of the House.

The Public Perception

1.   The House of Commons is at the heart of our democracy. The standards of conduct observed by its Members are crucially important to the political well-being of the nation. Those standards have always been self-imposed and self-regulated because Parliament is our supreme institution.

2.   It is vital for the quality of Government, for the effective scrutiny of Government, and for the democratic process, that Members of Parliament should maintain the highest standards of propriety in discharging their obligations to the public which elects them. It is also essential for public confidence that they should be seen to do so.

3.   In recent years the confidence of the public in politicians has declined sharply. Our first witness, Professor Ivor Crewe, told us that:

> *'Whenever surveys have asked people to compare various occupations for honesty or trustworthiness or a moral example, Members of Parliament have been at or near the bottom of the league, competing with estate agents and journalists to avoid the wooden spoon.'*

4.   He went on to mention a recent Gallup survey result that 64% of the public agreed that 'most MPs make a lot of money by using public office improperly', a figure which has risen from 46% nine years ago. The same survey found that 77% of people believed that 'MPs care more about special interests than about people like themselves', while only 28% agreed that ' most MPs have a high personal moral code'.

5.   Such figures must be treated with caution. On the suggestion that most Members of Parliament make a lot of money from using public office improperly, Professor Crewe told us 'I myself do not believe that for one moment'. Professor Crewe also told us that constituents would normally take a different view of their own Member. Iain Duncan-Smith MP, among others, agreed. He said:

> *'As politicians generally we are rated fairly low in people's regard [but] often you find that regard for an individual MP puts them high in the list of public perception within [the constituency]'.*

6.   There is no evidence either of a growth in actual corruption. When asked whether it was the considered judgement of the Metropolitan police that, whatever the problems with Members of Parliament accepting payment for lobbying services, these did not extend to corruption in the legal sense, Assistant Commissioner David Veness replied 'As of now that is correct.'

7.   John Witherow, Editor of 'The Sunday Times', and Peter Preston, Editor in Chief of 'The Guardian', both told us that they would not agree with the view that most Members were 'in it for the money', but nevertheless felt that public cynicism created a real problem. Not surprisingly, they took the view that this was Parliament's own fault, rather than the

media's. A comment by Lord Callaghan is relevant. Asked whether the House of Commons had turned its back on the strict approach of earlier years, he said:

> *'I think we have slipped into an easing of these sorts of arrangements rather than taken a deliberate decision about it, and our own standards, I think, have fallen into disuse in some ways.'*

8.   Members of Parliament themselves are aware of this loss of confidence, which to some extent reflects similar trends affecting democratic institutions elsewhere. Emma Nicholson MP told us:

> *'I think the sadness is that MPs feel that these great efforts that they make to help other people are no longer recognised and respected as such.'*

while Dale Campbell-Savours MP set out the issue succinctly:

> *'At the end of the day what do the public want? The public want to be assured that standards of propriety are being maintained—that is all.'*

Members' Financial Interests

9.   The reasons for the public's reduced confidence in the financial probity of Members of Parliament are not hard to identify. The public reads extensive press reporting of cases in which Members have accepted money for asking Parliamentary Questions, are said to have stayed at expensive hotels at others' expense without declaring an interest and are employed by multi-client lobbying firms, an attitude which has become known as 'MPs for hire.' Public confidence in MPs' overall standards of conduct has been further eroded by a regular flow of sexual revelations involving politicians.

10. It is harder to pin down precisely whether there has been an actual decline in the financial probity of Members. It would be surprising in a body of some 650 men and women if all had standards which were uniformly impeccable. There have been financial scandals in the past. The political historian, Lord Blake compared the present era with the Edwardian age when a 'get rich quick' mentality prevailed, and suggested that while the problems were worse at that time the present situation nonetheless gave rise to 'a good deal of unease'.

11. This unease undoubtedly has much to do with the growth of professional Parliamentary lobbying and the very substantial increase in the number of Members of Parliament employed as consultants and advisers to companies, trade associations and the like. Those with long experience of Parliament referred to the growth of lobbying and the problems it posed. For example, Chris Moncrieff, veteran lobby journalist, told us:

> *'Over the past four or five years there has been a massively increased influx of commercial lobbyist activity in the House of Commons and I think Members are far more vulnerable now than they have been ever before to outside and commercial pressures.'*

12. A number of witnesses pointed to another possible reason for increased commercial pressure on Members of Parliament. This is the relative decline in the pay of MPs and Ministers over recent years, and the greatly increased workload making MPs more likely to accept outside help. Alex Carlile MP said:

> '...it is a great honour and privilege to be an MP, but that does not feed, educate or clothe one's wife or husband and children'.

Sir Terence Higgins MP spoke of the workload, and also told us that in real terms average incomes in Britain were now 80% higher than when he entered the House in 1964, while the pay of MPs was the same and that of Ministers had declined by between 50% and 60%. Peter Thurnham MP, making a similar point, wrote of the extent to which he personally subsidised his constituency office:

> 'I found politics to be more demanding than I realised, with a commitment of over 100 working hours per week needed to defend a highly marginal seat through three general elections. ... I determined from the outset to establish a well staffed and equipped constituency office. ... Over the years this office has cost me a very substantial sum above the official allowances.'

13. Whatever the reason, there has been a significant growth in the number of Members of Parliament who have entered into consultancies or other forms of agreement which might reasonably be thought to influence their Parliamentary conduct. Analysis of the 1995 Register of Members' Interests suggests that 26 Members have consultancy agreements with public relations or lobbying firms and a further 142 have consultancies with other types of company or with trade associations. These 168 Members hold between them 356 consultancies. If Ministers and the Speaker are excluded there are 566 MPs. Thus almost 30% of eligible Members of Parliament hold consultancy agreements of these types.

14. A similar, though by no means identical, relationship which has of course existed for many years is that of sponsorship arrangements between Members and trade unions. The roots of trade union sponsorship go much further back into Parliamentary history than do those of modern consultancy. In the past, when Members were not paid, election to the House without such sponsorship would have been financially impossible for many Members. The importance of the financial link for the Member concerned may be less than it was. The financial support is generally limited to payment of a proportion of the Member's constituency office and election expenses. There is no remuneration for the Member personally. Yet it is only natural that it should give rise to feelings of obligation which have the potential to influence the Member's conduct in the House. According to the 1995 Register a total of 184 Members (over 30% of MPs excluding Ministers) have sponsorship arrangements with Trades Unions. In addition, 27 Members have paid consultancies with Trades Unions. A further 10 recieve other financial help from Trades Unions.

15. While the lack of detail in the Register makes precise analysis difficult, it appears in their different ways that some 389 of the 566 eligible MPs—almost 70%—have financial relationships with outside bodies which directly relate to their membership of the House. It is not surprising, therefore, that the financial question which gives rise to most public concern is the paid outside employment of Members.

16. The specific issues are these. Should any new restraints be placed on Members' freedom to take up outside jobs? If any outside employment is to be permitted how far can transparency protect the public interest? Are there circumstances in which a conflict of interest needs to be resolved by requiring a Member to withdraw from Parliamentary business? Do Members need further guidance? Can the public be confident that the rules on Members' interests are being firmly and fairly applied? We consider each of these in turn below.

Paid outside employment

17. A significant section of opinion holds that, as in certain other countries, Members of Parliament should have no outside paid interests, and that their only earned income should be their Parliamentary salaries. The majority of people who wrote to us took this view, as did Harry Barnes MP who gave oral evidence.

18. However most Members, journalists and business people from whom we heard took a different view. Ivor Crewe again told us that:

> '...a recent poll suggests that the public accept that MPs should be able to earn additional income from outside interests, so long as those interests are declared.'

while Tony Newton MP , the leader of the House of Commons, said:

> 'None of us would gain from a House of Commons made up of 651 people who were completely cut off from the rest of life, except on the basis of representations they received, rather than of experience of contacts they continued to have in various walks of life.'

19. We believe that those Members who wish to be full-time MPs should be free to do so, and that no pressure should be put on them to acquire outside interests. But we also consider it desirable for the House of Commons to contain Members with a wide variety of continuing outside interests. If that were not so, Parliament would be less well-informed and effective than it is now, and might well be more dependent on lobbyists. A Parliament composed entirely of full-time professional politicians would not serve the best interests of democracy. The House needs if possible to contain people with a wide range of current experience which can contribute to its expertise.

20. As well as having Members with continuing outside interests, it is important that the House of Commons should continue to contain Members from a wide variety of backgrounds. We should be worried about the possibility of a narrowing in the range of able men and women who would be attracted to stand for Parliament if Members were barred from having any outside paid interests. We believe that many able people would not wish to enter Parliament if they not only had to take a substantial drop in income to do so but also ran the risk of seeing their source of livelihood disappear altogether if they were to lose their seats. Several of our witnesses regretted the tendency for Members of Parliament to be drawn increasingly from those who have had no employment experience outside the political field.

21. The onward march of the professional politician may be an irresistible feature of modern life, but we believe that nothing should be done by way of institutional arrangements which would hasten it.

We recommend that Members of Parliament should remain free to have paid employment unrelated to their role as MPs.

Parliamentary Consultancies

22. A more specific issue then arises as to whether some paid outside interests are less acceptable than others. As we have noted above, the greatest current concern about the independence of the House arises when organisations seek the services of a Member of Parliament specifically as a Parliamentary adviser or consultant.

23. The need to protect the House against improper influences on Members has long been recognised. There is a statutory ban on Members holding various offices of profit under the Crown, including positions in the civil service and on the boards of publicly owned industries. The statutory position reflects the history of conflict between the monarchy and Parliament, and the fear that patronage could be used by the Crown to buy votes. It does not have much relevance to modern conditions.

Historical background

24. Although the same statutory prohibition as applies to public employment has not been extended to financial interests, concern about the influence of external financial pressures on Members, and the need to preserve their independence, is not new. In 1695, following the expulsion of Speaker Sir John Trevor for accepting a bribe of 1000 guineas from the City of London in connection with the Orphans Bill, the House resolved that 'the offer of money, or other advantage, to any Member of Parliament for the promoting of any matter whatsoever, depending or to be transacted in Parliament is a high crime and misdemeanour and tends to the subversion of the English constitution.'

25. In 1858 the House resolved that 'it is contrary to the usage and derogatory to the dignity of this House that any of its Members should bring forward, promote or advocate in this House any proceeding or measure in which he may have acted or been concerned for or in consideration of any pecuniary fee or reward.' This rule was specifically aimed at barristers.

26. By 1947 the position had not changed greatly. In that year the House declared that:

> '...it is inconsistent with the dignity of the House, with the duty of a Member to his constituency, and with the maintenance of the privilege of freedom of speech, for any Member of the House to enter into any contractual agreement with an outside body, controlling or limiting the Member's complete independence and freedom of action in Parliament or stipulating that he shall act in any way as the representative of such outside body in regard to any matters to be transacted in Parliament; the duty of a Member being to his constituency and to the country as a whole, rather than to any particular section thereof.'

27. In 1969 the Select Committee on Members' Interests (Declaration), known as the Strauss Committee, reviewed the rules on declaration of Members' Interests. While rejecting at that stage the concept of a Register of Interests, it proposed a new code of conduct for MPs. One arm of that code was a much stricter rule on declaration of interests. The other arm would have placed considerable restrictions on Members' freedom of action in the House in situations where they had financial interests. The Committee proposed that the House should adopt this resolution:

> *'That it is contrary to the usage and dignity of the House that a Member should bring forward by any speech or question, or advocate in this House or among his fellow Members any Bill, Motion, matter or cause for a fee, payment, retainer or reward, direct or indirect, which he has received, is receiving or expects to receive.'*

28. The Strauss Committee's report was never debated by the House, and their resolution was not adopted. In 1971 the then Leader of the House (Rt Hon William Whitelaw MP), clearly speaking following consultations via 'the usual channels', said:

> *'...following the Report there was very careful consideration of whether the Resolutions proposed would be suitable or would, in certain circumstances, be very much more restrictive than would be wise. It was felt that they would be so restrictive. ... there is widespread support in the House for the view that it is right to rely on the general good sense of Members rather than on formalised rules. That is certainly the view of the official Opposition.'*

The 1947 resolution and the rules of the House

29. The Strauss report did not therefore change the formal position. In principle this has remained unchanged for 50 years, and perhaps even for 300 years. The resolution of 1947 remains binding on Members of Parliament, and is the most detailed statement of the Law of Parliament on this subject. However this resolution, which appears at first sight clear and unequivocal, contains within itself the seeds of the current problem.

30. The 1947 resolution was drawn up in response to concern about an outside body—a trade union, as it happens—attempting to instruct a Member. It clearly prohibits any contracts which in any way limit a Member's freedom of action in the House. Thus it prohibits a Member from entering into a consultancy agreement which imposes, in return for payment, a binding obligation to speak, lobby or vote in accordance with the client's instructions, or to act as the client's representative in Parliament.

31. Although the resolution therefore prohibits a Member of Parliament from entering into any agreement requiring action on behalf of an outside body 'in regard to any matters to be transacted in Parliament', it does not prohibit a binding obligation to advise the client on Parliamentary matters. The Member remains free to enter an agreement to act as an adviser or consultant about Parliamentary matters. On the face of it therefore, this resolution might appear to draw the clear line between paid advice and paid advocacy which very many people, in Parliament and outside, have told us would be appropriate.

32. However the resolution does not prohibit Members from voluntarily speaking, lobbying or voting in support of their clients' interests if the Members think it right to do so, and if to do so is consistent with Members' duties to their constituents and to the public.

33. The voluntary nature of any action by the Member is important. No outside body would be able to use any financial arrangement with an MP to seek to secure any particular action in Parliament without committing a punishable contempt of Parliament. The Privileges Committee in 1946/47, in a passage which has been the basis of subsequent Privileges Committee reports, said:

> '... *if an outside body may properly enter into contractual relationships with, and make payments to a Member as such, it must in general be entitled to terminate that relationship if it lawfully can where it considers it necessary for its own interests to do so. What, on the other hand, an outside body is certainly not entitled to do is to use the agreement or the payment as an instrument by which it controls or seeks to control the conduct of a Member or to punish him for what he has done as a Member.'*

34. The rules of the House, therefore, as established over many years, focus very much on maintaining the privileges and freedom of action of Members, so that they cannot be compelled by outside bodies to act in a particular way in Parliament.

35. However the rules are much less explicit as regards restricting the freedom of Members to place themselves in situations where they are liable to be improperly influenced.

36. It is clearly established that it is an offence against the law of Parliament for a Member to accept a bribe. For lesser misdemeanours, however, the rules are much less clear. In the recent 'cash for questions' case, the Privileges Committee recommended action against the Members concerned on the basis that their conduct 'fell below the standards which the House is entitled to expect of its Members.' In his memorandum published in Volume II of the Privileges Committee Report, the then Clerk of the House (now a member of this Committee) stated:

> '*The House has never attempted to deal comprehensively with the potential conflicts of interest that can arise when the business and professional interests of Members touch upon their duties and responsibilities as Members. ... the House has preferred instead to deal with particular instances of conflict pragmatically when difficulties arise.'*

37. This position is entirely consistent with the 1971 statement of the then Leader of the House, referred to in paragraph 28 above, that 'it is right to rely on the general good sense of Members.'

Recent developments

38. Two major changes over the last fifty years have combined to concentrate attention on this latter area of Members' behaviour, and to bring into sharp focus the ambiguities left by the existing law of Parliament.

39. First, there has been a radical change in the nature of MPs' outside employment. Until recently, Members with paid outside employment typically pursued careers and occupations which, with the possible exception of journalism or the law, were largely unconnected with Parliament. Usually these were the same occupations that they had pursued before entering Parliament. Only a few Members were paid in connection with their Parliamentary duties. That position has now, however, been radically transformed. The proportion of Members pursuing careers largely unconnected with Parliament, such as farming, has fallen, while—as the figures in paragraph 13 above show—the proportion whose outside employment arises directly out of their Membership of the House of Commons has risen to a very significant level.

40. Second, the introduction of the Register of Members' Interests, designed to further the wholly admirable concept of disclosure of interests, has tended to create a false impression that any interest is acceptable once it has been registered, and so to add to the confusion which has developed.

41. Some of this confusion may stem from the 'defining purpose' of the Register as set out in the First Report of the Select Committee on Members' Interests 1991/92. This purpose is 'to provide information of any pecuniary interest or other material benefit which a Member receives which might reasonably be thought by others to influence his or her actions, speeches or votes in Parliament, or actions taken in his or her capacity as a Member of Parliament.'

42. In the 1995 edition of the Register of Members' Interests consultancy agreements come under the third of the listed categories of registrable interests. Under the heading 'clients' it provides that Members must disclose the names of clients 'for whom they provide services which depend essentially upon, or arise out of, Membership of the House; for example, sponsoring functions in the Parliamentary buildings, making representations to Government Departments or providing advice on Parliamentary or public affairs.'

43. The position is, therefore, that the 1947 resolution prevents a Member from agreeing to act for a client in Parliament, but the rules governing the Register of Members' Interests expressly contemplate that the Member may have received material benefits 'which might reasonably be thought by others to influence his or her actions, speeches or votes in Parliament' and which, in the case of consultancy agreements, may involve Members being paid for making representations to government departments on issues which inevitably will normally be concerned with matters to be transacted in Parliament.

44. The contrast between the 1947 Resolution and the rules governing the Register is in our view totally unsatisfactory. It is small wonder that it has given rise to confusion in the minds of Members of Parliament themselves. We agree with the comment made by Madam Speaker on 12 July 1994 (Official Report col 829) that there is an urgent need to clarify the law of Parliament in this area.

45. Although it is not comprehensive, the 1947 resolution is a clear statement of entirely sound principles. As a first step, therefore, we believe that it would clarify the position, and reinforce the impact of this resolution, if the House were to restate it at an early date.

The issues surrounding paid consultancies

46. The principal argument advanced in favour of allowing Members to put forward the views of their consultancy clients in Parliament is that many entirely respectable, and in some cases highly deserving, organisations can thereby gain a voice in the nation's affairs which would not be open to them by way of the normal constituency machinery. As a result, it is argued, the House as a whole is more fully informed and better able to debate the issues in question. Moreover, it is said, an imbalance is thus avoided between firms, professions and occupations whose members happen also to be Members of Parliament, and so can speak with authority on relevant subjects, and organisations such as trade associations, or charities, or the Police Federation which may be unable to command any such direct representation.

> *'If your Committee were to conclude that certain activities—for example paid advocacy on behalf of outside bodies—are incompatible with a membership of the House I would regard this as thoroughly helpful both to Members and to those, such as the Registrar, who have to advise them.'* Sir Geoffrey Johnson Smith MP
>
> *'I think for a Member to be a paid-up lobbyist is outrageous and I am amazed, if I may say so, that your confreres ever tolerated it...'* Simon Jenkins
>
> *'... we had no problem in deciding recently, when we first set up, that one of the first rules should be that we would not pay Members in any way whatsoever.'* Andrew Gifford, **President and founder of the Association of Professional Political Consultants**
>
> *'...we cannot have a situation where somebody only says something because they are paid, but nor can we have a situation where somebody does not say something even though they know more about it than anyone else.'* Ann Taylor MP
>
> *'I think there is a distinction between the advocates and the general advisers. But I think of the advocates, the lobbyist is by far the strongest and clearest example.'* Sir Norman Fowler MP
>
> *'The very word "lobby" implies promoting a cause in the lobby. It seems to me it is a very difficult relationship to regard with enthusiasm.'* Lord Howe
>
> *'There are some people who say they don't want a House of Commons full of professional politicians. Well I don't want a House of Commons full of part-time London lawyers, London journalists, London heart surgeons, City financiers or West End shop managers.'* Jeff Rooker MP

47. On the other hand, the consequence of the enormous growth in paid consultancy has been to create a real issue out of the distinction between paid advice and paid advocacy. Where once it might have mattered less that the occasional Member of Parliament who was

a paid adviser spoke in the client's interest in Parliament, this has become a matter of significant public concern.

48. If a Member is engaged to advise a client on Parliamentary matters affecting the client, and is at the same time free to speak, lobby and vote on those same matters in the House, it is not merely possible but highly likely that the Member will use Parliamentary opportunities in a way consistent with that advice.

49. It is more likely than not that Members who enter into consultancy agreements will do so with clients to whose viewpoints they are sympathetic, although Members who have such agreements have been at pains to tell us that they would not hesitate both to make clear to their clients where their views differed, and to express views in the House which their clients did not share. Nevertheless the impression can easily be gained, however unfair this may be in individual cases, that not only advice but also advocacy have been bought by the client. The evidence which we have received leaves us in little doubt that this is the impression which many people have. It is one of the most potent sources of public suspicion about the true motivation of Members of Parliament. In recent years Members have acquired paid consultancies on a large scale. Over the same period public scepticism about MPs' financial motives has increased sharply. It must be more likely than not that these two developments are related, but in any case their combination can only tend to undermine the dignity of Parliament as a whole.

50. We would consider it thoroughly unsatisfactory, possibly to the extent of being a contempt of Parliament, if a Member of Parliament, even if not strictly bound by an agreement with a client to pursue a particular interest in Parliament, was to pursue that interest solely or principally because payment, in cash or kind, was being made. A Member who believes in a cause should be prepared to promote it without payment; equally a Member ought not to pursue a cause more forcefully than might otherwise have been the case as a result of a financial interest. We believe that such action would breach the spirit if not the letter of the 1947 resolution, and we cannot be confident that all Members are as scrupulous in this respect as some have claimed to be.

51. With these factors in mind we have carefully considered whether we should recommend an immediate and total ban on all forms of advocacy in the House by Members pursuing the interests of those with whom they hold consultancy or sponsorship agreements. The effect of this would be to prevent Members with such interests from speaking, and perhaps from voting, when a relevant subject was under consideration. We have little doubt that such a ban would receive not only widespread public support but also support from many Members. A number of MPs who gave evidence to us endorsed the principle that paid advice is acceptable but paid advocacy is not. There is also a substantial body of opinion which holds that it is wrong in principle for Members to accept money for any services, even purely advisory services rendered in their capacities as Members.

52. We have concluded, however, that an immediate ban in that particular form, would be impracticable. It would involve asking three-fifths of the Members of the House and their clients or sponsors to amend with immediate effect arrangements which have been made perfectly lawfully and are often of very long standing. Because so many Members have such

interests, and so would be excluded from particular pieces of business, there would be a short term disruption of the business of the House. The impact on the income of many Members would have implications which could not be ignored. And the issues it would raise for the equilibrium of party political funding could only be addressed by a fundamental re-examination of that issue.

53. We have also concluded that further thought is needed before a firm decision can be taken on whether such a ban would be appropriate and on what the consequences would be of a decision to introduce such a ban. Parliament itself needs to debate further what it considers the Law of Parliament should be in this area. Parliament also needs to consider the implications for matters such as loss of income and party funding which are outside our terms of reference. Above all it needs to establish the facts. In this context, our recommendations below that agreements and remuneration in relation to Parliamentary consultancies should be disclosed in full are crucial. There is not sufficient information at present to enable a sound judgement to be made on whether the undoubted benefits of having well-informed and remunerated Members are outweighed by the risk of wealthy clients buying undue influence in Parliament.

54. While the further consideration suggested will need to be undertaken in some depth, and changes could take time to implement, the need to set the action in hand is urgent. The House may therefore think it right to hold an early debate with a view to commissioning the further work we propose. We ourselves will return to the subject in a year's time to review the position. In the meantime, individual Members may wish to consider whether in undertaking Parliamentary consultancies they may not have unwittingly put themselves under an obligation to advocate specific causes in Parliament in a manner contrary to the spirit, if not necessarily the letter, of the 1947 Resolution.

General consultancies

55. There is one area where we have no doubt that immediate action can and should be taken. Whatever arguments there may be in favour of Members who are retained as consultants by outside organisations acting as principals in their own right, we can see no justification for consultancy agreements between Members and public relations or lobbying firms, which are themselves acting as advisers and advocates for a constantly changing range of miscellaneous and often undisclosed interests. Similarly, it seems to us inappropriate for Members who are connected with legal and other professional firms which offer clients Parliamentary services of any type to retain that connection unless arrangements can be made to separate completely the Member's interest in the firm from that part of its work. We consider that this is precisely the situation which the Prime Minister has described as 'a hiring fair'. We believe that the House should act immediately to stop this practice by outlawing agreements which commit Members to giving Parliamentary advice for payment to multi-client lobbying organisations or to the clients of such organisations. We also believe that the House should prohibit Members from maintaining direct or active connections with firms, or those parts of firms, which provide paid Parliamentary services to multiple clients.

Immediate practical measures

56. We also believe that, whatever the longer term decision on consultancies, a package of practical measures should be introduced as soon as possible. These will clarify how Members with outside interests should behave in order to avoid conflicts of interest. We believe that they will remove the area of doubt about the law of Parliament, and so be helpful to Members. We also believe that they will restore public confidence that Members of Parliament are not being improperly influenced by outside financial interests. The measures we set out below combine strong re-affirmation of the existing rules of the House; more effective disclosure of relevant interests; better arrangements for preventing conflicts of interest, including a Code of Conduct for Members; better guidance on and more equitable enforcement of the rules, involving the creation of a new officer of the House.

57. We are well aware that some will consider that we are over-reacting to a few isolated cases, and that the individual judgement of Members of Parliament can be relied on. Others will feel we should have gone further, and moved immediately to recommend statutory controls.

58. It is clear that, while some cases have been so bad as to require direct action even under the existing rules, there are problems of principle and practice over the separation of public and private interests, which damage the standing of Parliament. Neither we nor the media have invented the problems. The House itself has recognised them and has made efforts to respond to them over the last quarter century. But the 1969 Strauss report was shelved without debate; the introduction of a Register of Interests was resisted until the Poulson scandal forced the hand of a new government in 1974; it has taken Members 20 years to accept the Register fully, with senior Members even in recent years feeling free to defy a Resolution of the House in respect of entries in the Register; and doubt has been expressed about whether justice has always been done to Members whose conduct has been judged by the House in recent years. While we accept that in the recent 'cash for questions' case the Privileges Committee has acted firmly, and that this should be fully recognised, the long-drawn out preliminaries to the committee's hearings were not such as to promote public confidence. The overall picture is not one of an institution whose Members have been quick to recognise or respond to public concern.

59. On the other hand we do not believe that the position is so grave that it has to be addressed outside the framework of the House's own rules. The question is whether the House is prepared to clarify and to implement those rules fully and objectively. An elected representative has a unique position, but it cannot be assumed that this inevitably makes that person's judgement of the balance of public and private interest infallible. The House collectively has a responsibility to safeguard the public interest against the possible misjudgment of individual Members, and it has the ability to do so. It also needs to reassert forcefully to the public that Members of Parliament, collectively and individually, have a sense of both the responsibilities and the dignity of the role with which they are entrusted. We believe that the House can do this itself, and that the package which we set out below will help it to do so. It is a powerful and flexible mixture of disclosure and enforcement which will serve the public interest better than the inflexibility of statutory procedures.

We recommend that the House should restate the 1947 resolution which places an absolute bar on Members entering into contracts or agreements which in any way restrict their freedom to act and speak as they wish, or which require them to act in Parliament as representatives of outside bodies.

We recommend that the House should prohibit Members from entering into any agreements in connection with their role as Parliamentarians to undertake services for or on behalf of organisations which provide paid Parliamentary services to multiple clients or from maintaining any direct or active connections with firms, or parts of larger firms, which provide such Parliamentary services.

We recommend that the House should set in hand without delay a broader consideration of the merits of Parliamentary consultancies generally, taking account of the financial and political funding implications of change.

We recommend that the House should:

- **require agreements and remuneration relating to Parliamentary services to be disclosed;**

- **expand the guidance on avoiding conflicts of interest;**

- **introduce a new Code of Conduct for Members;**

- **appoint a Parliamentary Commissioner for Standards;**

- **establish a new procedure for investigating and adjudicating on complaints in this area about Members.**

The detailed proposals for immediate action are set out in the following paragraphs.

Disclosure of interests

60. The House has for long operated on the principle that transparency is in most cases the best safeguard against conflicts of interest. Sir Terence Higgins MP said in evidence to us:

> *'Transparency is all important; wherever one draws the line on the issues you are considering, it is vital that there should be proper registration and it should be apparent both to the public, the House and Members themselves whether a person has an interest or not.'*

61. When the Register of Interests itself was established in 1974, it did not supersede the practice of declaring an interest at appropriate times. In fact the House in setting up the Register took the opportunity to enshrine in a formal resolution the long-standing convention of declaring an interest:

'In any debate or proceeding of the House or its Committees or transactions or communications which a Member may have with other Members or with Ministers or servants of the Crown, he shall disclose any relevant pecuniary interest or benefit of whatever nature, whether direct or indirect, that he may have had, may have, or may be expecting to have.'

This requirement casts its net wider than the Register, and it is not clear that its extent is always fully appreciated.

62. The House already goes to some lengths to ensure that Members of Select Committees know when to declare an interest. Declarations are required when putting a question to a witness and at deliberative meetings of the Committee. In addition, the Chairman is expected to seek declarations of interest immediately after the Committee is established, and to remind Members of their obligations from time to time.

63. There is much to be said for more systematic action to remind Members of their obligations to declare interests at other times. It is particularly important to emphasise that this obligation exists on each and every occasion when a Member approaches other Members or Ministers on a subject where a financial interest exists. Such contacts are often informal and private, and are therefore where the greatest risk of impropriety arises. It is clear that declaration at present is not always made in accordance with the rules, often through forgetfulness or misunderstanding. We have been told that Ministers always know when a Member who approaches them has a financial interest. But that is unlikely, especially given the number and extent of Members' financial interests. In any event the onus is on the Member to declare, not on the Minister to know. A Minister who discovers that an interest exists which has not been declared ought normally to consider whether the omission is sufficiently serious to report to the Select Committee on Members' Interests.

64. It has been suggested by some of our witnesses that the Register of Members' Interests is not particularly effective because it gives the appearance of declaration while permitting a form of declaration which may yield little information as to the true nature of the interest.

65. We agree. While the new 1995 register is an improvement on earlier editions, it lacks a standardised form of description and the nature of the interest is often difficult to discern. It is important that the Register should give a clear picture of the nature of the interest in question, and in particular of the nature of any activity that a Member is undertaking for payment, in order that a possible conflict of interest can be readily discerned. This is needed in respect of all declarable interests. At the same time, registration of minor interests, which obscure the real purpose of the register, should be discouraged.

66. Full declaration is especially important in respect of paid activities related to Parliament. We consider that in those cases, because the risk of impropriety is greater, it is essential that the full terms of all consultancy and sponsorship agreements, if not already in writing, should be reduced to writing and deposited along with the Register, so as to make them open for public inspection in full.

67. The need to deposit the contract in full is illustrated by the recent 'cash for questions' case. At several places in the evidence there is discussion of the form of entry which would have been put in the Register, and it is clear that whether or not payment was being made for a single question, or for a consultancy, the entries would have been wholly uninformative. One example will suffice. The Cash for Questions Report* contains the following exchange. Mr John Morris says:

> '… *Mr Calvert asks "How much information will you have to give when…" You reply: "What I shall say is something like this. I would put 'July 1994, consultancy project carried out for Mr Jonathan Calvert." '*

Mr Riddick responds:

> '*May I point out that that this is how the Registrar had suggested to me that I register this.'*

68. The Registrar is not blamed for suggesting an uninformative description, because the Member did not go into detail with him. But it is clearly unsatisfactory that such opaque descriptions are routinely being entered so that there is disclosure in appearance but not in practice.

69. Depositing the agreement will inevitably involve disclosure of the remuneration. We believe that the public, and in particular Members' constituents, have a right to know what financial benefits Members receive as a consequence of being elected to serve their constituencies. We consider it right, therefore, that remuneration should be disclosed in these cases. We also believe that information about the remuneration or other financial consideration received by a Member for Parliamentary services, or by way of sponsorship, should be entered in the register itself, possibly in banded form. It has been argued that actual remuneration is irrelevant, and that the mere existence of a financial relationship is what matters. That argument is not at all convincing. A Member who gets £1000 a year as a Parliamentary adviser is less likely to be influenced by the prospect of losing that money than one who receives £20,000 a year. The scale of the remuneration is in practice relevant to a full understanding of the nature of the service expected. We have noted that several MPs with whom we raised this issue did not object to disclosure of remuneration so long as this related strictly to Parliamentary services.

70. We are aware that in a number of other countries the practice is to require full disclosure of assets and income. But it is by no means clear that full disclosure of financial matters unrelated to Parliamentary business is relevant to the public interest. No-one has put a convincing case to us as to why that might be necessary.

On disclosure we recommend:

- **the Register should continue broadly in its present form, and should be published annually. However the detailed entry requirements should be improved to give a clearer description of the nature and scope of the interests declared;**

---

*   Committee of Privileges Report, Volume II, page 25, Q233.

- **updating of the Register should be immediate. The current updated version should be made more widely available electronically;**

- **from the beginning of the 1995/96 session (expected in November) Members should be required to deposit in full with the Register any contracts relating to the provision of services in their capacity as Members, and such contracts should be available for public inspection;**

- **from the same time, Members should be required to declare in the Register their annual remuneration, or estimated annual remuneration, in respect of such agreements. It would be acceptable if this were done in bands: eg under £1,000; £1,000–5,000; £5,000–10,000; then in £5,000 bands. An estimate of the monetary value of benefits in kind, including support services, should also be made;**

- **Members should be reminded more frequently of their obligations to Register and disclose interests, and that Registration does not remove the need for declaration, and better guidance should be given, especially on first arrival in the House.**

71. In addition, Members with employment agreements (including Directorships and Partnerships) which are unrelated to their role as Members, and which under our proposals would not therefore have to be deposited, should be advised to ensure that those agreements do not imply that they will perform any activities related to their Parliamentary role. Such action is necessary to reduce the risk of misunderstandings.

We recommend that Members should be advised in their own interests that all employment agreements which do not have to be deposited should contain terms, or be supported by an exchange of letters, which make it clear that no activities relating to Parliament are involved.

Lobbyists

72. Mention has been made in evidence to us of a proposal for a Register of Lobbyists. We are not attracted by this idea. It is the right of everyone to lobby Parliament and Ministers, and it is for public institutions to develop ways of controlling the reaction to approaches from professional lobbyists in such a way as to give due weight to their case while always taking care to consider the public interest and the interests of the constituents whom Members of Parliament represent. Our approach to the problem of lobbying is therefore based on better regulation of what happens in Parliament.

73.   To establish a public register of lobbyists would create the danger of giving the impression, which would no doubt be fostered by lobbyists themselves, that the only way to approach successfully Members or Ministers was by making use of a registered lobbyist. This would set up an undesirable hurdle, real or imagined, in the way of access.

74.   We commend the efforts of lobbyists to develop their own codes of practice, but we reject the concept of giving them formal status through a statutory register.

Conflicts of interest

75.   Disclosure of interests clearly goes a long way to reducing the risk of impropriety. But even when an interest has been disclosed, it may still be necessary in the public interest for the person with the interest to withdraw from the business in question.

76.   Such a procedure is now universal in government, local government and other public bodies, and common in the private sector. People with an interest must declare it, often withdraw from meetings, and take no further part in the business. In local government, following Poulson, failure to do this may be an offence.

77.   The Select Committee on Members' Interests has considered this issue on more than one occasion. In a report published in 1992*, it responded to suggestions that Members should be subjected to similar rules by saying:

> *'Comparisons are often drawn between the position of Members of Parliament and that of local authority councillors. These should be treated with caution. There are significant differences of function between the two.'*

78.   The Committee went on to quote with approval a witness who stated that all Members had an interest in all areas of public policy and must be allowed to participate in their deliberation, adding that the local government solution, if strictly enforced, would bring the work of the House to a halt. It then said:

> *'we heard ingenious arguments suggesting that there was little real distinction between the duties of Ministers of the Crown and the duties of other Members and proposing that both should comply with variants of the same rules. We did not find these arguments convincing. There is a world of difference between the position of Ministers, who have the responsibility for initiating policy and for taking executive decisions, and backbench Members, the powers of whom (as individuals) are confined to the exercise of influence.'*

79.   On this basis the Committee went on to conclude that full and public disclosure of relevant pecuniary interests was sufficient, and suggested that the only occasion on which a Member should withdraw from business was when the possibility arose of making private gain as a result of access to information:

---

*   Select Committee on Members' Interests, Session 1991/92 First Report. Registration and Declaration of Members' Financial Interests.

'As we have pointed out in an earlier report, if some Members, such as Chairmen and Members of Select Committees, acquire privileged insight into the development of policy they must expect that public opinion will eventually require that they should abide by rules which prevent them from holding particular interests or which require their withdrawal from certain proceedings.'

80. In fact, the Committee had understated the strength of the position adopted in its previous report*. That report, which was adopted on 13 July 1992 in a Resolution of the House, said:

'We feel that it is right that when a Member of a Committee, particularly the Chairman, has a pecuniary interest which is directly affected by a particular inquiry, or when he or she considers that a personal interest may reflect upon the work of the Committee or its subsequent report, the Member should stand aside from the Committee proceedings relating to it. This convention is so fundamental to the proper conduct of select committee business that we recommend that it should be reinforced by an appropriate resolution of the House.'

81. It has long been accepted that Members should not take part in Private Business in which they have a pecuniary interest, and there is one recorded case of Members being prevented from voting in Public Business in such circumstances. The 1992 Resolution extends the principle of requiring Members to withdraw from Public Business to cases where the pecuniary interest 'is directly affected' by a particular inquiry or where 'a personal interest may reflect upon the work of the Committee or its subsequent report.'

82. This was an important and welcome development, in that the House recognised that the public interest could be a factor in determining whether a Member should withdraw. However we agree with the Select Committee's 1992 comment that the position of Members is not entirely analogous with Ministers or local councillors, and that there are many areas of Parliamentary business where following a declaration of interest a Member can still make a valuable, and quite proper, contribution to public business. What is still needed is further guidance to Members on the appropriate action in differing situations.

83. There can be few cases where any damage to the public interest can result from a Member who has declared an interest speaking in the House, even in a Second Reading Debate of a relevant Bill or in a Committee of the whole House. And there is little risk of damage to the public interest at large, as opposed to the risk of damage to the credibility of Members of Parliament, when a Member who has a financial interest signs an early day motion, votes at a Division of the whole House, or puts down a Parliamentary Question, so long as the interest is declared on every occasion in the appropriate way. We believe that arrangements should be devised, possibly through the use of symbols on the Order Paper, to achieve this: it is already done for the proposers, though not other signatories, of Early Day Motions.

84. But there are other circumstances when the public interest may well demand that a Member with a financial interest should stand aside. In addition to the Select Committee position which the House has already addressed (see paragraph 80 above), the question of

---

*   Select Committee on Members' Interests, Session 1990/91 First Report.

Standing Committees needs to be considered. A Member who takes part in Standing Committee on a Bill is one of a small group which shapes the legislation in detail, some of whose amendments may well be accepted by government.

85. There will be circumstances where a Bill is sufficiently relevant to a sectional interest to make it against the public interest for Members with a financial interest to serve on such a Committee. In at least one recent case it has been suggested to us that the House failed to appreciate the risks of such a conflict of interest, to the possible detriment of the final legislation. This was the Cable Bill Standing Committee, when several Members of the Committee had financial interests, which they declared, in the industry in question. At present the House's own practice increases the risk, because it is customary for the Committee of Selection to make appointments to a Standing Committee from among those Members who have expressed a willingness to take part, and to reflect the balance of contributions in the Second Reading debate. This practice needs to be amended to incorporate a presumption against appointing Members with a financial interest.

We recommend that the rules and guidance on avoiding conflict of interest should be expanded on the lines we have suggested to cover the whole range of business pertaining to Parliament, and that particular attention should be paid to Standing Committees.

A Code of Conduct

86. Two recurring themes throughout our oral evidence were, first that any line drawn in order to ban particular Parliamentary activities by Members would give rise to anomalies, and second that the elected representatives of the people need to be trusted to exercise their own judgement. A comment by Lord Callaghan illustrates the point:

> *'I regard the sense of propriety of a Member of Parliament himself as to what he should do as being the ultimate test. … I hope you will be able to draw up a set of principles of conduct that will govern Members' financial interests. I would suggest that the Code, when drawn up and accepted by the House, should be adopted afresh by the House of Commons at the beginning of every Parliament after a general election...so that every new Member would understand what was expected of him and what was the normal code of behaviour.'*

87. We have suggested above a number of firm rules, and have also indicated a number of areas where difficulties arise. We share the view of those who warn against unduly detailed and prescriptive rules, but we also consider that it is unreasonable to expect that the view of every Member of Parliament of what is and is not acceptable will produce without guidance a universally acceptable standard.

88. While "Erskine May's Parliamentary Practice" is a thorough guide to the procedures and rules of Parliament it is a very weighty document, and we doubt that it is closely read by all Members. We believe therefore that more needs to be done in future to ensure that new Members are fully aware of all the rules on conflict and disclosure of interest, through induction sessions, a code of conduct and the preparation of guidance.

A Draft Code of Conduct for Members of Parliament

General Principles

It is the personal responsibility of every Member of Parliament to maintain those standards of conduct which the House and the electorate are entitled to expect, to protect the good name of Parliament and to advance the public interest.

Members should observe those general principles of conduct which apply to all people in public life. [These are set out on page 14 of this report, and should be incorporated into the final code]

The primary duty of Members is to their country and their constituents. They should undertake no actions in Parliament which conflict with that duty.

Because Members of Parliament enjoy certain privileges in law, which exist to enable them to fulfil their responsibilities to the citizens they represent, each Member has a particular personal responsibility to comply fully with all resolutions and conventions of the House relating to matters of conduct, and when in doubt to seek advice.

Financial Interests

A Member must not promote any matter in Parliament in return for payment.

A Member who has a financial interest, direct or indirect, must declare that interest in the currently approved manner when speaking in the House or in Committee, or otherwise taking part in Parliamentary proceedings, or approaching Ministers, civil servants or public bodies on a matter connected with that interest.

Where, in the pursuit of a Member's Parliamentary duties, the existence of a personal financial interest is likely to give rise to a conflict with the public interest, the Member has a personal responsibility to resolve that conflict either by disposing of the interest or by standing aside from the public business in question.

In any dealings with or on behalf of an organisation with whom a financial relationship exists, a Member must always bear in mind the overriding responsibility which exists to constituents and to the national interest. This is particularly important in respect of activities which may not be a matter of public record, such as informal meetings and functions.

In fulfilling the requirements on declaration and registration of interests and remuneration, and depositing of contracts, a Member must have regard to the purpose of those requirements and must comply fully with them, both in letter and spirit.

89. The Code of Conduct should provide a framework against which acceptable conduct should be judged, but should not contain excessive detail. It should avoid the type of detailed rules which can give rise to anomalies, but should set out principles clear enough to enable appropriate decisions to be made. It ought to be supplemented by detailed guidance from time to time. We believe too that the proposal that such a Code should be restated and debated early in the life of every new Parliament has much to commend it. We have set out our suggestion for a Code on page 39, and we commend this to the House, but we believe, in line with best practice in the private sector, that such a Code is more effective if the institution to which it is to apply draws it up and is committed to it.

We recommend that the House should draw up a Code of Conduct setting out the broad principles which should guide the conduct of Members, and that this should be restated in every new Parliament.

Enforcement of obligations

90. Because the House of Commons is responsible for enforcing its own rules, we regard it as a matter of concern that over recent years the procedures for their enforcement have appeared to be less than satisfactory. Proceedings related to conduct of Members in general have been carried forward on an ad hoc basis. Given the inevitable tendency for party politics to influence decisions on matters of conduct it is even more important for Parliament, the highest court in the land, to have established procedures which operate as a matter of course rather than chance. The public needs to see that breaches of the rules by its elected legislators are investigated as fairly, and dealt with as firmly, by Parliament in such cases as would be the case with others through the legal process. The recent arguments over how to conduct proceedings in the 'cash for questions' case point clearly to the need for fixed and fair arrangements which provide for proper investigation and demonstrably fair hearings.

91. Parliamentary Privilege is designed to ensure the proper working of Parliament, and is an essential constitutional safeguard. In the recent report on the 'cash for questions' case, the Committee of Privileges helpfully defined both its role and the concept of privilege:

> *"It may be helpful to the wider public to describe briefly the role of this Committee. Having been directed to examine a matter by the House, our essential function is to take evidence on its behalf in order to advise Members generally on whether and to what extent there appears to have been a breach of the privileges of the House or any action amounting to a contempt and to make recommendations to the House. It is for the House in all cases to take the final decision. Partly through precedent and partly by statute the House has over the years obtained certain rights known as "privileges". Their purpose is not to protect individual Members of Parliament but to provide the necessary framework in which the House in its corporate capacity and its Members as individuals can fulfil their responsibilities to the citizens whom they represent. Parliament defends it privileges by the law of contempt".*

92. One of the consequences of privilege is therefore that the House of Commons regulates the activities of its Members itself. Where Parliamentary business is concerned, they are answerable to the House and not to the Courts. Because Parliamentary privilege is important for reasons entirely unconnected with the standards of conduct of individual Members of Parliament, we believe that it would be highly desirable for self-regulation to continue.

93. For self-regulation to continue successfully, however, it is essential that Resolutions of the House—in effect the legal framework which the House imposes on its own operations—should be regarded as binding by all Members, and should be firmly, promptly and fairly enforced. Comments in evidence by Sir Geoffrey Johnson Smith MP, Chairman of the Select Committee on Members' Interests, illustrate the problem:

> *'I feel sure that the rules [on registration of interests] are now better understood by Members and more widely accepted by them than was the case some five or ten years ago. ... Some Members, when [the register] was introduced, did not quite understand the force of it. ... I used to spend some part of my time going round and reminding Members that they had not yet signed the register'*

94. Sir Geoffrey added that on occasion in the past he had to threaten to report a Member to the House, but that the Register was now accepted and this was no longer necessary.

95. In more recent years a number of senior Members did not accept a resolution of the House in respect of the Register, and refused to comply with it. In due course it was changed to meet their concerns. Yet when Parliament passes a law with which some people disagree, the expectation is that that law will be enforced until its opponents succeed in getting it changed.

96. We give this as an example. But there are other instances too which lead us to believe that Resolutions of the House in matters of conduct are not perceived by all Members as having the same impact as laws or regulations, even though they are the law of Parliament. In part this is because the House as a whole, and in consequence its staff, is clearly reluctant to sit in judgement on fellow Members unless a matter is very serious.

97. Such an attitude is entirely understandable, but wrong. Unless obligations are routinely and firmly enforced a culture of slackness can develop with the danger that in due course this could lead on to tolerance of corruption.

98. While we share with Chris Moncrieff the view that:

> *'Members of Parliament, generally speaking, are not corrupt and are well intentioned...',*

we firmly believe that the House of Commons needs to develop and implement a culture in which Resolutions of the House are automatically regarded as binding on Members, where there is a certainty of action when there is a breach of the rules, and where the procedures are fair and well understood. We believe that if the rules are clear, and enforcement is certain, the overwhelming majority of Members of Parliament will readily embrace and adhere to the standards which the House requires.

99. We consider that this can best be taken forward by combining a significant independent element with a system which remains essentially self-regulating. We believe that this should be done by appointing an officer of the House, called the Parliamentary Commissioner for Standards, to take responsibility for advising Members on, and playing an independent role in the enforcement of, the House's rules in respect of Members' conduct. If the House accepts our recommendation that a Code of Conduct should be drawn up, the Commissioner would take on the task of advising on that and producing guidance. We believe this would be helpful to Members themselves. Ann Taylor MP told us:

> *'It really is remarkable how, when Members of Parliament are first elected, they don't actually get a guide to the House of Commons which tells them the rules: just as there is no job description of a Member of Parliament, there is no set of rules which you are given once you arrive and by which you must abide.'*

100.   Mrs Taylor accepted the need for an element of independence in enforcement, as did a number of other witnesses, including Lord Howe and Roy Hattersley MP. Professor Sir William Wade, the leading constitutional lawyer, wrote to us as follows:

> *'The question is how breaches...should be adjudicated. Traditionally the House has been jealous of its privilege of self-regulation, but some Members have now proposed that there should be an independent element so as to eliminate political bias. In my opinion that would be a very desirable step. It would add to the reputation of the House and be well worth the surrender of privilege. Comparison might be made with election petitions, which until 1868 were decided by the House itself, but after that date were transferred to election courts manned by High Court judges, much to the benefit of justice.'*

101. We do not believe it is necessary to rehearse in detail the weaknesses of the present arrangements, but Lord Callaghan, John MacGregor MP (a former Leader of the House) and Sir Geoffrey Johnson Smith MP (Chairman of the Committee on Members' Interests) all commented on this. John MacGregor said:

> *'I have become concerned about the extent to which the Select Committee on Members' Interests is asked to be judge and jury, working out the evidence and so on. The procedures of the Select Committee may not be appropriate where there are serious issues affecting a Member's total career. ... For example, a Member is not entitled to question witnesses who are putting the case against him. I therefore feel that there is a case for having outside involvement in a Select Committee when it is dealing with such matters.'*

102.   We consider that our proposals to appoint an independent Commissioner and to overhaul the entire disciplinary procedure for Members should be sufficient to achieve the necessary detachment without recourse to the courts or indeed any surrender of privilege. The recommendations set out below should enable Members to secure a fair, thorough and expeditious hearing without removing the jurisdiction of the House of Commons. We

should say, however, that among others John Biffen MP (a former Leader of the House), Lord Blake and Professor Dawn Oliver have told us in effect that such procedures should be put on to a statutory basis. If adopted, the test of whether our recommendations are sufficient, or further change is needed, will be their operation in practice.

103.   There is one area of conduct where a need already exists to clarify, and perhaps alter, the boundary between the courts and Parliament. Bribery of a Member, or the acceptance of a bribe by a Member, is contempt of Parliament and can be punished by the House. The test which the House would apply for bribery would no doubt be similar to that which would apply under Common Law. However it is quite likely that Members of Parliament who accepted bribes in connection with their Parliamentary duties would be committing Common Law offences which could be tried by the courts. Doubt exists as to whether the courts or Parliament have jurisdiction in such cases.

104.   The Salmon Commission in 1976 recommended that such doubt should be resolved by legislation, but this has not been acted upon. We believe that it would be unsatisfactory to leave this issue outstanding when other aspects of the law of Parliament relating to conduct are being clarified. **We recommend that the Government should now take steps to clarify the law relating to the bribery of or the receipt of a bribe by a Member of Parliament.** This could usefully be combined with the consolidation of the statute law on bribery which Salmon also recommended, which the government accepted, but which has not been done. This might be a task which the Law Commission could take forward.

On procedure we recommend:

- **the House should appoint a person of independent standing, who should have a degree of tenure and not be a career member of the House of Commons staff, as Parliamentary Commissioner for Standards**. The Commissioner would take over responsibility for maintaining the Register of Members' Interests; advising on the code of conduct and questions of propriety; have responsibility for preparing guidance and providing induction sessions for new Members on matters of conduct, propriety and ethics; and have responsibility for receiving complaints about and investigating the conduct of Members in this area. **The Commissioner should have the same ability to make findings and conclusions public as is enjoyed by the Comptroller and Auditor General and the Parliamentary Commissioner for Administration.**

- **the Commissioner should have independent discretion to decide whether or not a complaint merits investigation or to initiate an investigation**. An investigation by the Commissioner would be conducted in private. Following an investigation the Commissioner would again have discretion either to dismiss a complaint, to find it proved and agree a remedy with the Member concerned, or to find a case to answer and refer the complaint to a Committee of the House. The Commissioner would be expected to publish the reasons for dismissing a case after investigation, the finding and remedy agreed when it was being taken no further, and the report to the Committee when a case was being taken further;

- **the Commissioner should be able to send for persons, papers and records, and will therefore need to be supported by the authority of a Select Committee with the necessary powers.** To give the powers personally to the Commissioner would require primary legislation, and we do not believe that to be necessary at this stage;

- there has been hitherto considerable uncertainty about the respective roles of the Select Committee on Members' Interests and the Committee of Privileges in enforcing the rules in this area. **We consider that a sub-committee of the Committee of Privileges, consisting of up to seven very senior Members, would be the best body to take forward individual cases recommended by the Commissioner for further consideration. We recommend that such a sub-committee should be established.** The enlarged responsibilities envisaged for the Commissioner might make it possible for the Select Committee on Members' Interests to be dispensed with altogether, with any residual functions being transferred to the Committee of Privileges with its sub-committee. But this is a matter for the House to determine;

- **in view of the fact that there would be a prima facie case to investigate, we recommend that hearings of the proposed sub-committee should normally be in public. We also recommend that the sub-committee should be able to call on the assistance of specialist advisers and that a Member who so wishes should be able to be accompanied by advisers before the sub-committee.** The arrangements should be such as to enable all concerned to see that the rules of natural justice are being applied. **We recommend that the sub-committee should be given discretion to enable an adviser to act as the Member's representative at hearings.** In exercising this discretion, it would be appropriate for the sub-committee to follow these principles set out in Halsbury*.

'Factors which ought to be taken into account in exercising the discretion include the seriousness of any allegations made or any potential penalty, whether any points of law are likely to arise, the capacity of the particular individual to present his or her own case, whether it will be necessary to cross-examine witnesses whose evidence has not been disclosed in advance, any potential delay, and the need for fairness as between all persons who may appear.'

---

* Halsbury's Laws of England, Fourth Edition.

- Where a formal penalty is thought to be appropriate, we commend the practice adopted in the recent Privileges Committee report on 'cash for questions' for a specific recommendation to that effect to be included in the sub-committee's report;

- an advantage of establishing a Commissioner and a sub-committee to deal with conduct cases would be that minor cases could be handled with maximum despatch and minimum fuss. **As the sub-committee would report to the full Privileges Committee this would have the practical effect of giving the Member a right of appeal to that Committee. Only the most serious cases should need to be considered by the whole House.** We believe that it should not be necessary for the House formally to endorse every adverse finding by the Privileges Committee, although it might be appropriate in certain cases for a Member to make a personal statement of regret. More severe penalties, involving suspension and possible loss of salary (in practice the equivalent of a fine) would continue to require the authority of the whole House.

Chapter 3

The Executive:
Ministers and Civil Servants

Principal conclusions

There is a need for greater clarity about the standards of conduct expected of Ministers. The Prime Minister should draw up specific guidance on this subject, based on the principles set out in this report

Careful consideration should be given to ensuring that the most appropriate means are used for the investigation of cases of alleged impropriety affecting Ministers. Other than in exceptional circumstances, the general rule that advice from civil servants to Ministers should not be made public should apply in these cases

There should be a new advisory system regulating the employment taken up by ex-Ministers. The system should be based on the existing civil service rules and should be flexible and as transparent as possible, while protecting personal privacy

The new system of appeal for civil servants to the civil service commissioners proposed by the Government should be extended by introducing systems for handling confidential appeals within civil service departments and agencies. The civil service commissioners should report the details of all appeals which have been upheld to Parliament

The civil service business appointments system should be more open. It should be actively monitored to ensure that the rules are being observed and complied with. It should cover special advisers

Introduction

1.   While the backbench Member of Parliament has a good deal of influence, it is the executive—Ministers and civil servants—which plays the major role in the making and execution of policy. Ministers are accountable to Parliament and the public for the work of their departments and agencies; less publicly, senior civil servants may substantially influence the policy process. Both are likely to be the target of lobbying.

2.   Despite the great difference in their formal responsibilities and their public profile, standards of conduct of both Ministers and civil servants must be of the highest. Combined, they exercise power directly over the lives of their fellow-citizens. Whether that power belongs to a Secretary of State approving a contract worth many millions, or a benefits clerk handling a claim for a few pounds, the maintenance of public trust is essential.

3.   During the course of our work we have been made aware of circumstances in which public trust has been weakened. For example, many of our correspondents and witnesses have commented on the ease with which Ministers can obtain employment with commercial firms with which they have had connexions while in office; disquiet has been expressed about the private lives of some Ministers; serving and retired civil servants have suggested that initiatives designed to improve efficiency in the provision of public services, such as the next steps programme and the contracting-out of public sector functions, have put at risk established standards of conduct.

The Conduct of Ministers

4.   The public is entitled to expect very high standards of behaviour from Ministers, as they have profound influence over the daily lives of us all. The example they set is closely scrutinised by the public and the media. As Vernon Bogdanor told us, 'it is from Ministers that standards in public life must flow'.

5.   We believe that a response is needed to the increased media and public interest in standards of ministerial conduct. In principle this interest is welcome. Yet the media does not confine itself to the public life of Ministers. It reports their sexual behaviour, their private conversations and in some cases the activities of their children and relatives. It can be oppressive and intrusive: to the extent to which it involves those who are not in public life through choice, it is seldom justified by legitimate public interest.

6.   In our view, there is a significant difference between media coverage of sexual behaviour, and accounts of financial impropriety, unacceptable conflicts of interest, or other forms of misconduct in office. Financial misbehaviour in particular matters to us all, because it strikes at the very heart of that confidence which people must have in Ministers and the motives behind their decisions. The same cannot normally be said of sexual misconduct. It is true that the private lives of Ministers may occasionally be relevant to the performance of their public duties, for example when their private conduct runs directly

counter to some public policy, gives rise to embarrassing publicity, or involves a security risk. We do not, however, feel that there are rules which can usefully be made about the sexual conduct of Ministers in the same way as those which apply to their financial interests.

7.   The evidence we have heard and received does not indicate that the public believes that Ministers are implicated in widespread wrong-doing. It does, however, suggest that people would welcome greater clarity about the standards of conduct to be expected of Ministers and how these are enforced.

Questions of Procedure for Ministers (QPM)

8.   What guidance there is for Ministers on standards of conduct, as well as on procedural matters, is contained in Questions of Procedure for Ministers. In the context of the British constitution, QPM is a youthful document, dating from 1945 (although elements within it are older). For many years, Questions of Procedure was a confidential document. It was only in 1992 that the present Prime Minister took the decision to publish it.

9.   QPM has no particular constitutional status, but because it is issued by each Prime Minister to ministerial colleagues at the start of an administration or on their appointment to office, and any changes can only be authorised by the Prime Minister, it is in practice binding on all members of a Government. The records show that QPM has grown organically over the years, beginning as a document that was not much more than what Lord Trend described as 'tips on etiquette for beginners' but with fresh sections being added to deal with new circumstances. Over the years, the growth in QPM has largely been in the area of conduct and not procedure.

10.   We do not believe that the explanation for this is a decline in ministerial standards of conduct. We think that the addition of ethical material to QPM has resulted from a combination of responses to specific incidents and a general trend, not confined to Government, towards codification of what might once have been assumed to be common ground.

Ministers and the Prime Minister

11.   QPM begins by setting out some fundamental principles:

> *'It will be for individual Ministers to judge how best to act in order to uphold the highest standards. Ministers will want to see that no conflict arises or appears to arise between their private interests and their public duties. They will wish to be as open as possible with Parliament and the public. These notes should be read against the background of these general obligations'*.

12.   Ministers themselves are individually and separately responsible for upholding the standards of conduct applicable to their office. Everyone in public life has a personal responsibility for judging a course of action—the acceptance of hospitality, for example— weighing up its ethical implications using their own judgement. In the case of Ministers, their need to account to Parliament for their actions reinforces that responsibility.

---

*   Questions of Procedure for Ministers (Cabinet Office 1992), paragraph 1.

13. Yet Ministers do not make their ethical judgements in isolation. To remain in office they must retain the confidence of the Prime Minister and, in a question of conduct, that will involve the Prime Minister's own judgement of the ethics of the case. This is axiomatic and should be reflected in QPM.

We recommend that the first paragraph of Questions of Procedure for Ministers should be amended to say: 'It will be for individual Ministers to judge how best to act in order to uphold the highest standards. <u>It will be for the Prime Minister to determine whether or not they have done so in any particular circumstance.</u>'

Guidance to Ministers on Conduct

14. We believe that there are general principles of conduct which are applicable to Ministers; that it is possible to set these out in a clear and comprehensible form that will be of assistance to the Prime Minister, to Ministers themselves and to members of the public; and that this can indicate unacceptable aspects of ministerial behaviour. This approach will not, of course, stop misconduct. But it will do much to counter present public uncertainty about what is and is not acceptable.

15. QPM does not offer a coherent series of principles which can be applied by Ministers who are in doubt about possible courses of action. The document is a miscellany: 'a mix of immutable principles with housekeeping practicalities', as Professor Peter Hennessey described it to us.

We recommend that the Prime Minister puts in hand the production of a document drawing out from QPM the ethical principles and rules which it contains to form a free-standing code of conduct or a separate section within a new QPM. If QPM is to remain the home for this guidance, we recommend that it is retitled 'Conduct and Procedure for Ministers' to reflect its scope.

16. The precise wording of the new guidance will be a matter for the Prime Minister. We believe, however, that the following essential principles should be spelt out, supported where necessary by detailed rules, some of which already exist in QPM:

> *Ministers of the Crown are expected to behave according to the highest standards of constitutional and personal conduct. In particular they must observe the following principles of ministerial conduct:*
>
> *i)* *Ministers must ensure that no conflict arises, or appears to arise, between their public duties and their private interests;*
>
> *ii)* *Ministers must not mislead Parliament. They must be as open as possible with Parliament and the public;*
>
> *iii) Ministers are accountable to Parliament for the policies and operations of their departments and agencies;*
>
> *iv) Ministers should avoid accepting any gift or hospitality which might, or might appear to, compromise their judgement or place them under an improper obligation;*

> *v) Ministers in the House of Commons must keep separate their roles as Minister and constituency Member;*
>
> *vi) Ministers must keep their party and ministerial roles separate. They must not ask civil servants to carry out party political duties or to act in any other way that would conflict with the Civil Service Code.*

17.   Setting out these principles for Ministers might seem unnecessary or obvious. We do not share that view. The Government has accepted the proposition that there should be a code of conduct for civil servants. It is difficult to see why the same approach should not apply to Ministers. The advantages of a code can be seen by considering the number of Ministers who have had to resign since the war because of avoidable errors of judgement. We do not, though, believe that express sanctions need to be set out to prevent Ministers from doing wrong. Public and media scrutiny of ministerial conduct in the light of the principles we have listed above is likely to be far more effective. Ministers themselves will be able to judge possible courses of action against these principles, supported by the useful rules-of-thumb recommended to us by Lord Howe: 'Would you...feel happy to see all the relevant facts of any transaction or relationship fully and fairly reported on the front page of your favourite newspaper', and 'If in doubt, cut it out'.

Scrutinising Ministerial Conduct

18.   The way in which allegations of ministerial misconduct are dealt with will depend very much on the circumstances of each case. In the nature of things, such allegations may well be made publicly or become public. It is important for the public interest, the reputation of the Minister concerned, and that of the Government that allegations are investigated promptly and effectively.

19.   The handling of allegations of criminal misbehaviour is relatively straightforward. The police will investigate the alleged offence. It may be necessary for a Minister to stand down in these circumstances, but there is no ambiguity about the process of investigation. Fortunately, such cases are extremely rare. It is more common for allegations of misconduct to fall well short of criminal behaviour and to be concerned with sexual behaviour, conflicts of interest, or financial impropriety.

20.   Recent cases have shown that there may be circumstances in which the Prime Minister needs further advice or information. There are various people to whom the Prime Minister may turn for this. There is no reason why the advice of the Cabinet Secretary should not be sought on how best to proceed. Indeed it would be usual to do so, particularly if it is alleged that a Minister breached the principles of ministerial conduct in QPM. In some circumstances the preparation of advice may require investigation into the facts: this will depend on the nature of the case. However, if the allegations relate to past behaviour before entering office, or personal misbehaviour unconnected in any way with ministerial duties, they are not matters for the Cabinet Secretary, who should advise the Prime Minister to that effect.

21. It is impossible to foresee all the circumstances which then arise. In some cases, it may be a matter for the police, in others, for the Chief Whip or other ministerial colleagues, the security services or the Law Officers. In some cases, where Parliamentary rules are involved, the Prime Minister might refer the case to the proposed Parliamentary Commissioner for Standards. A very serious and complex case might merit a Tribunal of Inquiry. Occasionally a suitably qualified individual might be engaged to carry out an investigation. In a good many cases, an internal administrative investigation may suffice.

22. During or after any investigation, by whomever it is carried out, into a Minister's conduct, the Cabinet Secretary may well have to advise the Prime Minister, or (acting on the Prime Minister's behalf) to advise the Minister concerned on the best course of action to take in respect of his or her ministerial office. We believe that a clear distinction must be drawn between the report of an investigation, which it might be appropriate to publish, and the Cabinet Secretary's advice, which should never, or very rarely, be made public. The political impartiality of the civil service has to be protected, and it is wrong for such advice to become part of the debate over a Minister's behaviour.

We recommend that careful consideration should be given to ensuring that the most appropriate means is used for the investigation of cases of alleged impropriety affecting Ministers. We recommend that, other than in exceptional circumstances, the general rule that advice from civil servants to Ministers should not be made public should apply in these cases.

Employment After Leaving the Government

23. One aspect of the conduct of Ministers has been repeatedly raised in evidence to us: the absence of rules on employment after leaving public office. We have considered whether this is a justified area of concern. We have concluded that it is.

24. Ministers have the opportunity while in Government to take decisions which may favour or disadvantage outside bodies, including individual firms. For civil servants (and members of the armed forces) in a similar position, regulations have existed for many years to reassure the public that decisions made while in office have not been influenced by the prospect of employment after leaving the civil service. These rules, administered by an independent committee, are known as the business appointment rules. Although they are non-statutory, they are flexible, understood, and seldom disobeyed. Cabinet Ministers have much greater responsibility for decisions about Government policy than even the most senior civil servants. Yet Ministers can take any post they wish—subject to the dictates of their own consciences—whereas senior civil servants must have their plans approved for a full two years after the date of their departure from government service. That is difficult to justify.

25. We have heard arguments both in favour of and against the introduction of a business appointment system for Ministers. The Government's view was given by the Chancellor of the Duchy of Lancaster, David Hunt MP, who argued that 'it is still right to leave decisions about these matters to the judgement of the individuals concerned'. We recognise the force of some of the points which he made. We have also, however, to take into

consideration other evidence which we received, not least from former Conservative Ministers, people of considerable experience in public life. Sir Norman Fowler MP said that 'the aims of the civil service code seem to me … equally applicable to Ministers'. His view was shared by Lord Callaghan, Lord Younger, and many of our other witnesses. Sir Norman Fowler also pointed out that 'both the public and former Ministers would benefit from a clearly stated set of rules'. We agree. The risk of abuse, or of unfounded and malicious criticism, would be much reduced by a vetting system.

26.   It has been argued that in most cases, senior civil servants will leave public service at a retirement age which is known in advance, and that on departure most will receive a full pension. In the case of Ministers, their departure from government may be abrupt and their severance pay is likely to be very much less. Nevertheless, the same principles of public interest apply. The reassurance of the public that standards of conduct are being maintained is an overriding necessity. As Lord Younger said, 'Ministers have to take the rough with the smooth on this'. We have also taken note of the argument that a restrictive system will discourage talented people from becoming Ministers. In the commercial world, restrictions on freedom of future employment are normally compensated in the remuneration package, but we accept that this is unlikely to happen with Ministers. We consider, however, that the risk of discouraging candidates for ministerial office will be minimal if, just as with the civil service rules, any rules for Ministers are drawn so as to affect only the limited number of possible moves which give genuine reason for concern. Lord Carlisle, the Chairman of the Advisory Committee on Business Appointments, which advises on the application of the present rules, told us that approximately 70% of the cases put before his Committee attract neither waiting period nor other restriction. We have no reason to suppose that the pattern for ministerial applications would be very different.

27.   We share the view that there should be as much interchange as possible between the public and private sectors. The civil service rules restrict interchange between the sectors, but on a narrow and defensible basis. Ministers should be able to contribute their expertise and their knowledge of government to companies that wish to employ them, because the benefits to the country and economy may be substantial. A flexible system, which curtails employment plans only when they might threaten public confidence in standards of conduct, would not prevent those benefits from being realised.

The Civil Service Business Appointment Rules

28.   The salient points of the existing civil service business appointment system are as follows:

i)   all civil servants at grades 1 and 1A (permanent secretary) and 2 (deputy secretary) must submit their future job plans to the Advisory Committee on Business Appointments for approval, unless the job is unpaid and in a non-commercial organisation, or is a public appointment;

ii)   they must seek approval both for their first job and for any others within two years of leaving the civil service. Approval is given by the Prime Minister on the advice of the Advisory Committee;

iii) there is an automatic waiting period of three months imposed on all grade 1 and 1A (permanent secretary) civil servants, except fixed-term appointees;

iv) the advisory committee may recommend a waiting period of up to two years (from the date of leaving the civil service) before the ex-civil servant can take up the job, and may also impose what are called 'behavioural conditions'. These govern what the ex-civil servant may not do for his or her new employer: they may, for example, prevent ex-civil servants from contacting their former departments or working on tenders for Government projects. These conditions may also last for up to two years from the date of leaving Government service.

v) the rules are not designed to detect corruption, which would be a criminal matter. 'The aim of the application of the rules is to maintain public trust in [the civil and military] services and in the people who work in them'*;

vi) The advisory committee recommends whether a waiting period or behavioural condition should be applied under two headings. It considers whether a proposed move creates 'any suspicion, no matter how unjustified, that the advice and decisions of a serving officer might be influenced by the hope or expectation of future employment with a particular firm or organisation'. It also takes into account 'the risk that a particular firm might gain an improper advantage over its competitors by employing someone, who, in the course of their official duties, has had access to technical or other information which those competitors might legitimately regard as their own trade secrets or to information relating to proposed developments in Government policy which may affect that firm or its competitors.'*;

vii) the rules apply equally to civil servants below grade 2, although these cases are not normally dealt with by the advisory committee. Final decisions rest with departmental Ministers. Applications at Grade 3, and the more sensitive cases below Grade 3, must be referred to the Cabinet Office for advice.

A Ministerial Business Appointments System

29. The civil service system is tried and tested; our view is that it appears to be accepted by civil servants and it provides a strong reassurance to the public. Public concern now demands a similar reassurance in the case of Ministers. We believe that the evidence we have heard indicates that the civil service system, with some slight modifications, could be applied to Ministers.

---

* Civil Service Management Code 4.3 Annex A.

30. We have considered whether a Ministerial system should be enforceable by statute, or purely advisory. We believe that a transparent advisory system will achieve the necessary liberty of movement for individuals but nevertheless secure public confidence and ministerial compliance, without the complication of a statutory power. In other words, if ex-Ministers knew that a failure to seek the views of an advisory body or to abide by its advice would be reported in public, the fact that there were no legal sanctions would not matter. The threat of hostile public reaction and media comment would be a powerful disincentive. However, we would not rule out returning to this subject in the future, should practical experience convince us that a voluntary system was insufficient to sustain public confidence.

31. A purely advisory system places great weight on those advising. We have considered whether some form of new advisory machinery needs to be created which would be of sufficient standing and expertise to offer advice to Ministers. We do not feel that fresh arrangements are necessary. The existing Advisory Committee on Business Appointments draws its membership from senior retired politicians, civil servants, the diplomatic service and the armed forces. Its members have long experience in applying the rules sensibly and flexibly to senior civil servants and they are supported by a secretariat in the Cabinet Office. In principle, we see no reason why the advisory committee should not take on the task of advising Ministers on their future employment plans. We are confirmed in this view by the evidence given to us by Lord Carlisle, who said 'if you ask me whether [the advisory committee] could take on the task of advising Ministers, I think my answer must be yes'. The former Cabinet Secretary, Lord Armstrong, agreed. Among our own members are two members of the advisory committee who endorse that proposition.

We recommend that a system similar to the civil service business appointment rules should apply to Ministers. The system should operate on an advisory basis, and it should be administered by the existing Advisory Committee on Business Appointments.

32. Under the civil service system, permanent secretary grades (1 and 1A) are required to undergo an automatic three-month waiting period before taking up outside employment. We have heard no evidence in favour of abolishing that basic safeguard and have therefore considered whether this should also apply to Ministers. The automatic three months waiting period recognises the special position of permanent secretaries within the civil service and the breadth of their responsibilities. Similar considerations apply to Cabinet Ministers.

33. Under the civil service arrangements, two years from the date of leaving office is the maximum delay that can be applied and, except for permanent secretaries, there is no automatic waiting period. Is a similar maximum waiting period for former Ministers sufficient to allay public criticism? On the face of it, it seems that it may not be. Ministers have been criticised for joining companies which they have privatised, or which have advised them on privatisations, after intervals well in excess of two years. We feel that this criticism, while understandable given the many other firms which former Ministers might have joined, is nevertheless based on a misunderstanding of the function of the rules. Any

waiting period would be insufficient in a case of genuine corruption. Waiting periods are not punishments, but a means of maintaining public confidence. Neither do we feel that Ministers outside the Cabinet should be subject to automatic waiting periods. The circumstances of each case should determine the decisions of the advisory committee. That will help the new system attract the co-operation of those whose freedom of action it may impair.

We recommend that, in parallel with the civil service arrangements for permanent secretaries, an automatic waiting period of three months should apply to former Cabinet Ministers, but not to other Ministers or Whips. In cases where a further waiting period is recommended, the maximum waiting period should be set at two years from the date of leaving office.

34. We accept, however, that there may be rare situations which create such suspicion of impropriety that it would simply be better for the applicant not to proceed. In these circumstances, the advisory committee should be able to advise an applicant, whether a civil servant or a former Minister, that they feel that the application is not appropriate. If the applicant persisted, then a two-year waiting period would be imposed, and if the applicant then took the employment, the committee's comments on the wisdom of the application would become public in the normal way. In reality, we believe that the publication of the committee's advice, and the subsequent public scrutiny, would stop an unwise application in its tracks.

We recommend that the advisory committee should be able to advise an applicant, whether a civil servant or a former Minister, that they feel that the application is not appropriate, and to make public that advice if it is not taken.

35. No waiting period, of course, is free from anomaly. Under the civil service rules, civil servants can wait for two years and a day and take whatever employment they wish without the advisory committee being involved, although we have heard no evidence that this is done from improper motives. We have had to strike a balance between the rights of individuals and the need to reassure the public. We believe that requiring Ministers to seek the advice of the Committee for two years after leaving office, and a maximum waiting period of the same length, achieves those aims. We expect that Ministers who are in doubt about the propriety of an appointment after the two years has expired will continue to bear in mind the injunction in QPM 'that they should naturally avoid any course which would reflect on their or the Government's reputation for integrity or the confidentiality of its proceedings'*. If they remain in doubt about a particular offer of employment, we believe that they should be able to seek the advice of the advisory committee, even after the expiry of the two year period.

36. Under the present system, the advisory committee, as its name suggests, merely puts recommendations to the Prime Minister of the day who may vary the conditions or waiting periods which the committee applies, although this happens rarely. We do not feel, for reasons which have been pointed out by a number of witnesses, that the ministerial system could work in precisely the same way. It might seem invidious, for example, for Ministers

---

*   Questions of Procedure for Ministers, paragraph 105.

who have just been dismissed by the Prime Minister to have to submit their future employment plans to the same Prime Minister for consideration. On the other hand, to exclude the Prime Minister would deny Ministers any form of appeal.

We recommend that former Ministers, having received the advice of the advisory committee, should have the right of appeal to the Prime Minister of the day, who would be able to reduce any waiting period or relax any conditions if the appeal were well-founded.

37. If there were no appeal, then the Prime Minister would not be involved. We have considered whether a change of administration would make that appeal system unworkable, but we have confidence in the traditions of courteous relations between political opponents and see no reason to doubt that a Prime Minister of one party would deal fairly with appeals from the former Ministers of another.

38. As soon as a former Minister has taken up a job which the advisory committee has scrutinised, the committee should make public the advice it had given and its reasons. A summary of all cases dealt with that year should be subsequently published in an annual report. There would be no announcement if a Minister decided not to go ahead with an appointment after hearing the views of the advisory committee: that would be an unjustified intrusion into personal privacy.

We recommend that the system should be as open as possible, while protecting the personal privacy of Ministers.

39. Some concern has been expressed to us about the capacity of the present advisory committee and its secretariat to cope with the additional workload that would be generated by having to advise Ministers. In recent years the advisory committee has been asked to advise on between 34 and 48 cases per year, covering applications from Grade 1, 1A and 2 staff in the Home Civil Service and their equivalents in the diplomatic service and armed forces. The committee's secretariat has an internal target to put cases to the advisory committee within 5 days of receiving application forms from departments. If the applicant asks for a personal hearing in front of the committee, which happens in only a small number of cases, the secretary of the advisory committee told us that they are dealt with in three weeks. It is impossible to predict precisely what will happen if a ministerial system is introduced, but research carried out on our behalf* indicates that under normal circumstances the present advisory committee would be able to administer the new arrangements, although there might be consequences for the staffing of its secretariat. Maintaining the present rapid processing of cases will be important however, and in the special case of a general election leading to a change of government, there might well be a rush of applications.

We recommend that the Government should monitor the workload of the advisory committee under the new arrangements and put in place contingency arrangements for its staffing to be augmented to deal with the aftermath of any change of administration.

---

*   'Ex-Ministers' Business Interests 1979–94', research carried out by the Labour Research Department.

The Acceptance of Gifts and Hospitality

40. We have considered the rules on acceptance of gifts by Ministers set out in QPM (paragraphs 80–81) and are satisfied that they are sufficiently detailed. The rules on the acceptance of hospitality are necessarily less rigid, because of the difficulty of defining all possible circumstances. The principle set out in paragraph 126 of QPM is an important one:

> *'It is a well-established and recognised rule that no Minister or public servant should accept gifts, hospitality or services from anyone which would, or might appear to, place him or her under an obligation.'*

41. We have considered whether recent cases, in which Ministers have accepted hospitality or had their travel costs paid, indicate that this principle needs to be strengthened or clarified. We have concluded that additional detail is unnecessary. The rules are 'pretty clear' thought Lord Younger, and Lord Armstrong felt that more detail would encourage a legalistic approach. We believe, however, that it is important that the public should be reassured that standards of propriety are being maintained.

We recommend that departments, as well as maintaining records of gifts, should maintain records of hospitality accepted by Ministers in their official capacity and should make these records available if asked to do so.

Ministers who accept hospitality on the basis of personal friendship, involving accommodation or holidays, or other significant cost, should be advised to record that they have done so if they think there is any possibility that the failure to do so might otherwise be misunderstood or misrepresented.

42. Such a record would supplement the declarations made by Ministers who are Members of the House of Commons in the Register of Members' Interests, which requires the declaration of gifts above £125 in value, and hospitality if above £160 in value.

The Civil Service

43. As Giles Radice MP said to us, 'it is a priceless gift that we have an impartial, non-corrupt civil service'. The civil service is well provided with codes of behaviour, with detailed rules on conduct and with generally accepted principles which have been in place since the mid-nineteenth century. From 1854 until the late 1960s the civil service developed greater uniformity and tighter central control. In the 1980s, that process was deliberately reversed, with the establishment of executive agencies and the delegation from the centre of many management responsibilities. The question of standards of conduct was not much considered when those changes were made: the need for efficiency and effectiveness in the delivery of services was given pre-eminent place.

44. The remit of this Committee does not extend to reviewing the merits of particular ways of managing the civil service. Our concern is strictly with any developments which

might imperil long-standing rules of conduct and with how such threats might be averted without weakening the entirely proper drive towards better public sector management.

45. We believe that standards of behaviour in the civil service as a whole remain very high, and that cases of outright corruption and fraud are rare, although individual cases can be very serious. Nor have we received evidence that other important standards—political impartiality or the ideal of public service—are under systematic threat. We will, however, study with interest the conclusions reached by Sir Richard Scott in his inquiry into the export of defence equipment. If it appears that misconduct by civil servants was widespread or if the report raises general issues of propriety or impartiality, we may need to return to this subject in our future work.

46. Our task has been made much easier by two recent reports on the civil service. The Treasury and Civil Service Select Committee produced a perceptive and thorough analysis of many of the most pressing issues facing the civil service. The Government responded with a positive White Paper, 'Taking Forward Continuity and Change', reflecting the welcome degree of common ground that exists between the political parties about the future of the civil service*.

Core Values

47. In the White Paper, the Government restated and endorsed the core values of the civil service: 'integrity, political impartiality, objectivity, selection and promotion on merit and accountability through Ministers to Parliament'. We agree with the Government's view that 'with greater delegation and more movement in and out of the civil service, there is a need for even greater vigilance about standards throughout the civil service'. The Government lists four policies intended to help:

    i)   the establishment of a new senior civil service;

    ii)   a new handbook for agency chief executives;

    iii) a new civil service code;

    iv) an independent line of appeal for civil servants to the Civil Service Commissioners.

48. We welcome the establishment of a new senior civil service as a symbol of the importance of shared values throughout the whole civil service. We agree, however, with the view of some of our witnesses that caution should be exercised in the introduction of performance pay and appraisal arrangements for this group. Many, though not all, of the senior civil service will be in contact with Ministers and will handle sensitive policy matters. A perception that reward and promotion may depend in any way on commitment to Ministerial ideology inconsistent with the impartiality required of a civil servant would of course be wholly unacceptable.

We recommend that the new performance pay arrangements for the senior civil service should be structured so as not to undermine political impartiality.

---

*   Treasury and Civil Service Committee, Fifth Report, House of Commons 27, 1993–94, 'Taking Forward Continuity and Change', Cmnd 2748, 1995.

49. A guide for Agency Chief Executives on core values and standards properly responds, in our view, to the pressures which may occur when traditional public sector values are applied in an organisation with a sharper commercial focus, such as some executive agencies. However, we note here that the issuing of guidance and codes is not the end of the matter. We return to this in paragraph 61 below.

The Code and Appeal System

50. Devising a clear and brief code for civil servants setting out the constitutional framework within which they work is entirely in keeping with the principles which we have recommended in this report and we welcome it. We hope that it will be a helpful element in sustaining civil service morale. Well-motivated and self-confident organisations find it much easier to maintain good standards of conduct among their staff.

51. In order for the appeal to the Civil Service Commissioners to work effectively, two changes to the proposed code would be helpful. The present draft paragraph 11 envisages an appeal being made by a civil servant who has been asked 'to act in a way which is illegal, improper, unethical, or in breach of constitutional convention, which may involve possible maladministration, or which is otherwise inconsistent with this code or raises a fundamental issue of conscience'.

We recommend that the draft civil service code should be revised to cover circumstances in which a civil servant, while not personally involved, is aware of wrongdoing or maladministration taking place.

Similarly, paragraph 7 of the draft should be made more general by deleting the words underlined:

> 'civil servants should endeavour to ensure the proper, effective and efficient use of public money within their control'.

52. We are disappointed by the Government's proposal that the Civil Service Commissioners should report to Parliament only those cases in which the Government has failed to heed their recommendation. There seems to be no pressing constitutional reason for this limitation on openness. If the Commissioners were to report to Parliament in all cases when an appeal has been upheld, it would then be open for the Government to respond in public. This system has the great advantage that there will be no barrier to the dissemination of best practice arising out of the Commissioners' recommendations. The Government has already accepted this principle in the case of the Parliamentary Commissioner for Administration and the Public Accounts Committee.

We recommend that the operation of the appeals system should be disseminated as openly as possible, and the Commissioners should report all successful appeals to Parliament.

53. The institution of an independent appeals system is a step forward. We remain concerned, however, that the minimal use made of the previous appeal mechanism to the

Head of the Home Civil Service (only one appeal in eight years) may be replicated under the new system because of the requirement that all internal avenues of appeal must be exhausted before the Civil Service Commissioners become involved. As Lord Armstrong observed, 'I don't know that an appeal to the First Civil Service Commissioner is any less intimidating than an appeal to the Head of the Home Civil Service'. What we believe is needed is a parallel system allowing staff to raise concerns in confidence without necessarily having to take them through the management structure in the first instance. We believe that departments and agencies should nominate one or more officials entrusted with the duty of investigating staff concerns raised confidentially. Such a person must stand outside the line management structure of the complainant but should expect and receive the support of senior management when investigating alleged abuses. The limits of the person's powers of investigation should be set out on the lines of those laid down for the Commissioners in the new civil service code (amended, as we propose, in paragraph 51 above).

We recommend that departments and agencies should nominate one or more officials entrusted with the duty of investigating staff concerns raised confidentially.

54. We recognise that this represents something of a novelty, although the use of confidential appeal systems and hotlines is not uncommon in the private sector. Structured in the way we suggest, however, such a system could be introduced within the framework of the constitutional conventions governing the work of civil servants and their relations with Ministers. We accept the Government's view that most issues can safely be resolved by the normal mechanisms within departments and agencies. We think, however, that the prevention of corruption and maladministration is hampered if an individual civil servant has to identify him or herself as a complainant before superiors who may have direct influence over his or her career. That has been found to be a powerful disincentive to 'whistleblowers' in other organisations. The independent charity, Public Concern at Work, has set out Good Practice Guidelines which recommend that employees are offered confidential routes to raise concerns*. Indeed, the result of failing to provide a confidential system for matters of conscience is, ironically, to encourage leaks, which are damaging to the cohesiveness of civil service bodies and weaken the relationship between Ministers and civil servants.

A Civil Service Act

55. The Government has begun a process of consultation on whether the civil service should no longer be regulated under the Prerogative but should be the subject of a narrowly drafted statute. We see merit in the idea of a statutorily based civil service, provided that a consensus can be reached between the parties as to the scope of the legislation.

We recommend that the new civil service code should be introduced with immediate effect, without waiting for legislation.

---

* Public Concern at Work, First Annual Report (1994), page 12.

The code should not itself appear in primary legislation, which would make it difficult to amend in the light of changing circumstances. Instead, it should be contained in secondary legislation subject to the affirmative resolution of both Houses, ensuring that flexibility is joined with scrutiny.

56. We acknowledge the force of the government's argument that any such legislation should not alter the constitutional basis for the civil service or confer on civil servants special rights over and above those of other employees.

Political Misconduct

57. From time to time there have been allegations, repeated by witnesses at our inquiry, that civil servants were being asked by Ministers to undertake duties which were not appropriate to their non-political status, such as writing constituency speeches or supplying MPs with pro-Government parliamentary questions. It has also been suggested that some civil servants have allowed themselves to become so publicly partisan and enthusiastic about Government policies that it would be difficult for them to retain the confidence of any incoming administration of a different political colour. No evidence was offered to us that these are other than isolated cases. The existing guidance offered both to Ministers and civil servants has always been clear on the point that there is a boundary beyond which a civil servant should not be asked, or volunteer, to go. We have recommended as an additional safeguard (paragraph 16 (vi) above) that guidance for Ministers should spell this out more clearly.

Conduct in the Civil Service

58. We turn now to the detailed arrangements governing conduct in the civil service. Under the Civil Service Management Code (CSMC), departments and agencies are given delegated powers to introduce regulations on conduct, so long as they reflect the principles and rules set out in CSMC. The principles in CSMC cover, among other things, the need for civil servants to be seen to be honest and impartial in the discharge of their duties. In particular, civil servants must not misuse official information; must not do anything which compromises their political impartiality; and must not use their official position to further their own interests. CSMC also contains the rules on business appointments and on political activity.

59. The detailed departmental and agency regulations which derive from these principles are held to form part of a civil servant's contract of employment, and breaches can be the subject of disciplinary action. The process of delegation creates the possibility that, over time, detailed rules on conduct might diverge, depending on the circumstances of the department or agency making them. The Cabinet Office has therefore recently carried out a survey and discussion of the operation of these rules, intended to promote best practice.

We recommend that the Cabinet Office should continue to survey and disseminate best practice on maintaining standards of conduct to ensure that basic principles of conduct are being properly observed.

60. Central statistics on disciplinary cases in the civil service are no longer collected. We therefore carried out a survey of our own, to which 82 departments and agencies responded, covering disciplinary cases between 1989 and 1994. The results did not demonstrate any significant increase in any category of disciplinary case over the period. We are however concerned to note that comparatively few departments or agencies felt it worthwhile to draw the attention of their staff to the rules on conduct, other than by issuing an annual circular or office notice. Even fewer bodies had attempted to survey their staff to determine what awareness existed of their codes and what understanding there was of the principles underlying them.

61. We find this regrettable. Commercial organisations which have gone through what is called 'de-layering' have recognised that increased management responsibility at lower levels may confront junior staff with ethical issues of which they have had no previous experience. They may need support which is no longer provided by the line management hierarchy. The civil service is increasingly in the same position and at the same time is being asked to become more flexible and entrepreneurial in its provision of services.

We recommend that there should be regular surveys in departments and agencies of the knowledge and understanding staff have of ethical standards which apply to them; and that where such surveys indicate problem areas, guidance should be reinforced and disseminated appropriately, particularly by way of additional training.

The Business Appointment Rules

62. In paragraph 28 above, we summarised the salient features of the business appointment rules. We suggested how they might be applied to Ministers. We now turn to their operation in respect of civil servants. About 1,000 applications a year are examined by the advisory committee, the Cabinet Office, or departments. The advisory committee deals with applications made by civil servants in Grades 1 and 2. The Cabinet Office deals with all cases at grade 3, or at more junior grades where the applicant has had significant dealings with the prospective employer and conditions are likely to be required. The remainder are handled by departments. Of the 1,000, about 300 are handled centrally, and waiting periods or conditions are recommended for some 30% of these. The comparable figure for waiting periods or conditions for the 700 or so cases handled in departments is about 20%.

63. The Treasury and Civil Service Select Committee has examined the operation of the business appointment rules in detail on a number of occasions, most recently in 1991*. It is their view that on the whole the system works well and achieves the appropriate balance between reassuring the public and permitting civil servants (and other Crown servants) to move freely into the private sector where there is no perception of impropriety. Sir Robin Butler described the system to us as offering 'a reasonable balance'.

64. We have recommended for Ministers that a maximum two-year restraint on taking up outside appointments is normally adequate. We believe that the same applies to the civil service. We have however recommended in paragraph 34 above that the advisory committee should have the power to recommend to applicants—whether Ministers or civil servants—that they should not proceed with an unwise application.

---

* Fourth Report 1990–91, 'The Acceptance of Outside Appointments by Crown Servants'.

65. At present, applications under the business appointments system remain confidential. We have recommended in the case of Ministers that the system should become open (except in the case of applications which are not followed up) and that the advisory committee should give reasons for its decisions. The Government has consistently argued in the past that openness would not be appropriate for the present system and said in written evidence to this Committee that 'if it was known that details of all applications and the decisions made on them were routinely made public, it is likely that employers would be inhibited from opening discussions with those affected and employees would be reluctant to make applications'.

66. We agree that there is no reason based on public confidence why speculative applications made by civil servants should be made public. We do not, however, accept that the disclosure of decisions in individual cases is wrong in principle once the appointment has been taken up. The system is designed to maintain public confidence in the conduct of individual public servants. It is contradictory to keep details secret and to expect the public to take on trust the application of the rules. We were reinforced in that view by our witnesses Elizabeth Symons, Lord Armstrong, and Lord Carlisle, none of whom saw any objection to openness about applications after the employment has been taken up. If a civil service union leader, the former head of the civil service, and the chairman of the advisory committee are of one mind, we find their testimony very persuasive.

We recommend that the Advisory Committee on Business Appointments should, when an appointment has been taken up, give the reasons for its decision in that particular case.

It would be unnecessarily time-consuming for cases at lower grades routinely to be published in that way. However, departments and agencies (and the Cabinet Office, for centrally determined applications) should be ready to give such information on demand.

67. In order to comply with our recommendation, those who administer the system will need to be in a position to know whether the applicant has taken up a post. Applicants to the advisory committee should therefore be asked to notify it when they take up an appointment which has been the subject of an application.

68. It is a striking weakness of the existing system that there is at present no monitoring of its effectiveness. Although the rules are considered binding on all civil servants, no attempt is made to track, even on a sample basis, conformity with decisions taken by departments, by the Cabinet Office, or by the advisory committee. We have been made aware during our work of cases of failure to apply under the rules although the proposed employment fell well within their scope. From time to time departments become aware by chance of failures to apply and retrospective applications may then be made. Although we accept that in the vast majority of cases the rules are complied with and the decisions which flow from it are observed, it is damaging to public confidence in the system for this state of affairs to continue. It would however be unrealistic and unjustified to expect all movements out of the civil service to be monitored.

We recommend that the operation, observance and objectives of the civil service business appointment rules should be reviewed.

This would be a suitable subject for an inter-departmental efficiency scrutiny team, which can build on the work that is currently being done on the operation of the rules in the light of the changing pattern of civil service employment. Thereafter, occasional sampling of compliance with the rules should be undertaken.

69. One group of civil servants remain entirely outside the scope of the existing rules: special advisers. Special advisers are civil servants but, like Ministers, may lose their posts with little or no warning. Because in theory they are not permitted to have access to details of individual companies or to become involved in the placing of contracts or other work that requires an application under the rules, they have been exempted. However, the rules are not limited to these circumstances. Applications have to be made 'to avoid the risk that a particular firm might gain an improper advantage over its competitors by employing someone who, in the course of their official duties, has had access...to information relating to proposed developments in Government policy which may affect that firm or its competitors'*.

70. Special advisers probably have a better knowledge of proposed developments in Government policy than most other civil servants in their departments, and it is not easy to see why they should be exempt from the rules. If Ministers are brought within the system, as we recommend, then the anomaly is even more obvious.

We recommend that special advisers should be subject to the business appointment rules.

The Acceptance of Gifts and Hospitality

71. We are satisfied that the rules relating to the acceptance of gifts by officials are sufficiently strict and rather tighter than those which apply to Ministers. In most departments, officials are not allowed to accept more than trivial gifts, while Ministers can accept gifts up to a current value of £125 so long as they are declared. Although there might be a logical case made for relaxing the civil service rules in respect of officials who are not involved in the award of contracts, on balance we consider that the present strict rules on gifts should continue.

72. As for hospitality, for officials generally we see advantages in their continuing to be free to accept invitations to working lunches and dinners, and for those with a representational role to attend other events. We understand that in most departments either a central or local record is kept of such invitations and acceptances, and it is specified that management must be consulted about hospitality which is in any way disproportionate, frequently repeated, or otherwise unusual.

We recommend that a central or local record of invitations and offers of hospitality accepted is kept in all departments and agencies. There should be clear rules specifying the circumstances in which staff should seek management advice about the advisability of accepting invitations and offers of hospitality.

---

*   Civil Service Management Code 4.3 Annex A, paragraph 3(b).

Chapter 4

Quangos
(Executive NDPBs & NHS bodies)

Principal conclusions

Appointments

Appointments to the boards of executive NDPBs and NHS bodies should be made on the basis of merit, to form boards with a balance of relevant skills and backgrounds.

Responsibility for appointments should remain with Ministers, advised by committees which include independent members.

A Public Appointments Commissioner should be appointed, to regulate, monitor, and report on the public appointments process.

The process should be open and departments should have to justify any departures from best practice. Job specifications should be published, and a wide range of candidates should be sought. The suitability of each candidate should be assessed by an advisory committee.

Propriety

It should be mandatory for each executive NDPB and NHS body to have a code of conduct for board members, and a similar code for staff.

A review should be undertaken by the Government with a view to producing a more consistent legal framework governing propriety and accountability in public bodies including executive NDPBs, NHS bodies and local authorities.

Openness and independent monitoring are important safeguards of propriety, and should be extended. In particular staff should have a confidential avenue to raise any concerns about issues of propriety.

The responsibilities of accounting officers for propriety as well as financial matters need to be emphasised. Audit arrangements should be reviewed to ensure that best practice applies to all public bodies.

Introduction

1.   During our enquiries we encountered a range of concerns about "quangos" (quasi-autonomous non-governmental organisations). In this report we examine in particular the questions of:

- whether appointments are being unduly influenced by party political considerations;

- whether there is sufficient openness both in the appointments process and in quangos' proceedings;

- whether enough is done to maintain standards of propriety.

After a brief review of the factual information about quangos, our discussion and recommendations on the appointments process are at paras 16–72, followed by those on safeguards to ensure propriety at paras 73–126.

2.   We also heard concerns about a perceived increase in the number of quangos; and about a lack of democratic accountability. Some felt that lines of accountability through Ministers to Parliament were too strained to be meaningful, particularly in the case of local bodies. We do not seek to address these issues, which are essentially about the principle of "government by quango". Whether functions are carried out by government departments, by local authorities, by quangos or by any other means is an issue of public policy rather than a matter of standards of conduct. Similarly the merits of underlying policies, such as the internal market reforms in the NHS, are not for us to consider. These issues are the subject of intense political debate and are likely to remain so.

3.   The use of quangos is not unique to Britain, nor is it a recent practice. A survey of 250 'fringe bodies' in 1978 found that 10 had been set up before 1900 and 84 before 1949. Few of the submissions we have received expressed doubt that such bodies can play a useful role. They perform functions at arm's length from the day to day running of central government, their members often contributing unique specialist knowledge and wider experience to public life.

What is a quango?

4.   There is no universally accepted definition of a quango. The government uses the term "Non-Departmental Public Bodies" (NDPBs) of which there are three major types:

- Executive bodies: which between them carry out a wide range of operational and regulatory functions, various scientific and cultural activities and some commercial or semi-commercial activities.

- Advisory bodies: which are usually composed of a group of experts in a particular sphere advising the government on one narrow issue.

- Tribunals: which, as their names suggest, have a judicial or quasi-judicial function.

5.   The annual Government publication 'Public Bodies' includes information on NDPBs and NHS bodies. The 1994 edition lists a total of 1,345 NDPBs of which 325 are executive bodies spending £15bn of public money. Since 1979 there has been a decline in the total number of NDPBs. The number of executive bodies has also declined, although their expenditure has risen in real terms by around 75%. (See Table 1) Departmental expenditure in support of all bodies including advisory bodies and tribunals is a further £170m. By far the bulk of expenditure is therefore by and on behalf of executive bodies. 'Public Bodies' also lists over 600 NHS bodies spending a further £25bn.

Table 1: Non-Departmental Public bodies 1979–94

| | | Executive NDPBs | | |
Department	Total number of NDPBs	Number	Public expenditure (current prices)	Public expenditure (1994 prices)
1979	2,167	492	£2.97 billion	£8.51 billion
1994	1,345	325	£15.08 billion	£15.08 billion

Source: Public Bodies 1994

6.   There are wider definitions of "quangos" in use, which usually include local bodies which are independent or self governing, but which spend public money and perform public functions. In many cases these functions were previously provided by national or local government. This includes bodies such as Training and Enterprise Councils (TECs), Local Enterprise Companies (LECs) in Scotland, Housing Associations, Further Education Corporations and the Boards of Grant Maintained Schools. The members of such bodies are not appointed by Ministers, although their membership is usually regulated either by statute or in contracts with government.

7.   A study* by the Democratic Audit of the United Kingdom, a research unit based at the University of Essex, suggested a total of up to 5,500 executive "extra-governmental organisations". At 1992/93 prices, they estimated that such organisations spent £47bn compared to £35bn in 1978/79. The National Audit Office told us that expenditure by NDPBs and other bodies receiving significant public funds totalled £52bn in 1993/94.

8.   Public Bodies 1994 lists over 42,000 appointments made by Ministers of which perhaps 10,000 or so are renewed each year (see Table 2). This includes around 8,800 positions on executive NDPBs and NHS bodies.

Table 2: Summary of Public Appointments at 1st September 1994

Executive Bodies	3,850
NHS Bodies	5,015
Advisory Bodies	10,065
Tribunals	21,973
Boards of visitors	1,782
Nationalised Industries	104
Public Corporations	87
Total	**42,876**

Source: Public Bodies 1994

---

*   Ego-trip: Extra-governmental organisations, in the United Kingdom and their accountability', edited by Weir S. & Hall H., published by the Charter 88 Trust, 1994.

9.   Only about 37% of all public appointments receive remuneration other than travelling expenses and only 0.5%—around 170 posts—are paid more than £50,000 a year. In the NHS, where all non-executive members of trusts and health authorities are paid (mostly at a flat rate of £5,000 a year), the proportion receiving pay rises to 93%. Levels of pay should be strictly controlled and consistent with the responsibilities involved, but we accept that on some boards, particularly in the NHS, these responsibilities are now much heavier than they may have been in the recent past. Nevertheless, many people still give valuable service either without recompense or at a much lower rate of pay than their skills could attract elsewhere. The tradition of voluntary public service is still clearly alive, and we believe it is important to strengthen and preserve it.

10.   Government policy in recent years has been to move away from larger "representative" boards to smaller "corporate" boards whose members are appointed as individuals rather than as representatives of a particular interest or viewpoint. In the NHS, the number of non-executive appointments is expected to decline from 6,500 in 1990 to 3,500 by 1996, although the functions and expenditure they control will roughly remain the same. At the same time, public sector management reforms have delegated greater management and financial freedom to individual public bodies. As a result each quango member is seen to hold greater personal power and influence, and inevitably this heightens concerns about who they are, how they are appointed and how they behave.

Focusing our work

11.   Our terms of reference cover all these bodies. For this first report, however, we have concentrated on two areas:

- executive Non-Departmental Public Bodies; and

- National Health Service bodies, principally health authorities and trusts.

12.   **Annex 1** lists the main bodies. Within the limits imposed by the number and diversity of bodies, even within this more limited field, we have sought to establish principles which will be widely applicable.

Appointments

Present arrangements for appointments

13.   Each Government Department is responsible for making its own appointments to executive NDPBs and NHS bodies. The role of the central departments—the Treasury and the Office of Public Service & Science (OPSS) in the Cabinet Office—is limited to issuing guidance and maintaining a list of potential candidates.

14.   The Public Appointments Unit (PAU) in OPSS produces a comprehensive 'Guide to Public Appointments Procedures', which includes mandatory requirements for advising Ministers; advice on maintaining candidate lists/databases, advertising, executive search

consultants and interviewing; examples of good practice; and sources of additional information.

15. The PAU seeks nominations, including self-nominations to its list, using a standard application form which asks for particular areas of interest, referees and a CV. It produces a leaflet on the process; holds seminars with representative organisations; and has recently begun a formal rolling programme of writing to business, trade union, professional and party organisations inviting nominations. Departments are recommended to consult the PAU list when making appointments, but they are not required to do so, and in practice only a small proportion of appointments, are filled in this way*. The majority of departments also maintain their own lists, and some produce their own guidance.

The Government's recent reviews

16. An inter-departmental review of these arrangements, co-ordinated by the PAU, was presented to us as part of the Government's evidence. It found that, despite the common central guidance, actual procedures varied widely. There were many examples of good practice, but other areas and departments where procedures were less thorough. The PAU review recommends a strengthening of the guidance, and the promotion of good practice to bring all procedures into line with the best. This includes measures to:

- improve the transparency of the process, by documenting procedures and recording the reasons for decisions by Ministers and officials;

- widen the range of methods used to obtain candidates, including a presumption in favour of advertising and the use of executive search where appropriate;

- achieve greater openness, by announcing appointments and making lists of appointees available to the public;

- increase the rigour of the process, through the routine use of references and interviews;

- ensure standards of probity through the early identification of potential conflicts of interest.

A summary of the recommendations, with our comments on them, is at **Annex 2**.

17. New government guidance on appointments to health authorities & NHS trusts in England was also presented to us. It proposes the greater use of advertising and other methods to widen the field for appointments. It sets out clear job descriptions, lists the qualities sought in NHS non-executives, and institutes a more formal sifting mechanism for recommending candidates to Ministers, with an optional independent member on the sifting panels. A summary of the NHS proposals with our comments on them is at **Annex 3**.

18. Both reviews are very welcome developments. We support the proposed changes, which go a considerable way towards meeting current concerns and remedying existing defects. The remainder of the section on appointments addresses those issues which fell

---

* Answers from 11 departments to PQs from Tony Wright MP identified 84 posts filled in this way in 1992, although this excludes the departments appointing to NHS bodies who did not hold central records.

outside the remit of these reviews (such as whether Ministers should continue to make appointments), issues where our views were expressly sought (eg. on the declaration of political affiliation or office-holding) and areas where we believe the recommendations could be strengthened or clarified (particularly the provision of advice to Ministers, and the proposed mechanisms for monitoring and scrutiny). We do not set out to repeat all the minor points included in the Annexes.

Who appoints?

19. The final selection of candidates by Ministers was taken as given in both the Government's reviews. Our terms of reference are wider, and we consider first of all whether the responsibility for making appointments should remain with Ministers or whether some or all appointments should be transferred to an independent appointing body. The key questions are these. Is there an endemic political bias in appointments by Ministers? Do appointments represent an unhealthy concentration of the power of patronage in very few hands? Should some or all appointments be made by an impartial and independent body?

20. Appointments to executive NDPBs and NHS bodies are the subject of considerable political debate. We heard suggestions from many of our witnesses and correspondents that a disproportionate number of posts are given to Conservative party activists, ex-candidates or those who have donated money to the party, both as a reward for loyalty and as a way of ensuring boards who will be supportive of Government policies and uncritical of Ministerial decisions.

21. Other witnesses, including Sir Norman Fowler, Lord Armstrong, Alan Langlands and David Hunt, argued that public appointments had not been politicised. Some, such as Archie Kirkwood MP, agreed that there was little or no evidence of systematic bias, but rather a tendency for Ministers to appoint those who were closest to them, especially where there was felt to be a need to fill new posts quickly. Sir Norman Fowler, among others, gave us examples of cases where previous administrations had tended to appoint their sympathisers to public posts. It was pointed out by several witnesses that most public appointments, far from being a reward, represent a considerable personal commitment by the individuals appointed and often some financial sacrifice.

22. Although the perception of bias has become quite widespread, the evidence is circumstantial and inconclusive. When they reviewed the range of available studies for us, researchers at the Institute of Local Government (INLOGOV) at Birmingham University concluded that these studies tended to suggest that individuals who are Conservative Party supporters, or whose companies make donations to the Conservative Party, are more likely to be found on appointed bodies than people who support the Labour or Liberal Democrat parties. The studies did not, however, clearly demonstrate political bias in the making of appointments.

23. Any discussion of alleged political bias shades into a debate on the types of skills and personal qualities which are sought in the appointments system. The current focus on business skills might result in appointees who are naturally more likely to be Conservative

party supporters. On the other hand, a variety of our witnesses suggested that, in the interests of good government, Ministers had to appoint people who were sympathetic to the policies they were implementing, and this inevitably left an impression of political bias where none existed. We discuss this issue in more detail at paras 37–40.

24. It is also clear that most studies start from a definite pro- or anti-quango stance. Taken as a whole, we find the available research and other evidence insufficient to support a conclusion. As several studies point out it is often hard to fully determine the truth or otherwise of individual allegations as detailed information about how the appointment was made is rarely available (see paras 59–63 on openness).

25. Nevertheless, it is clear that Ministers exert considerable powers of patronage. They make or approve up to 10,000 appointments each year, including over 2,000 appointments to executive NDPBs and NHS bodies. Some argue that this is an unhealthy concentration of power, particularly given the limited checks on the exercise of that power which exist at present. If decisions are not made on a personal and party basis—or even on caprice and whim—it is largely because of the good sense of those in office, rather than because the system prevents such abuses. We share some of this concern, particularly about the absence of independent checks and balances, not least because suspicions of bias remain nearly impossible to prove or disprove. The resulting uncertainty does not provide solid ground on which to build public confidence in the system.

26. One way of allaying such concerns would be to give the responsibility for making appointments to an impartial and independent body. An analogy can be made with the civil service. Appointments made by departments and agencies are overseen by the Civil Service Commissioners, with the Commissioners themselves taking a direct role in the more senior appointments. On the other hand, it is argued that, in order to retain accountability to Parliament, a Minister must retain responsibility for making appointments and, where problems arise, for terminating them.

27. Proponents of an independent appointing body find it problematic to devise an appropriate means of democratic scrutiny. Tony Wright MP supported such a body but saw difficulties in giving the House of Commons a direct role in major appointments as its "partisan character will always triumph over its collegiate character". We did not feel that any of our witnesses or correspondents had presented a convincing proposal for providing public accountability other than through the established route of Ministerial accountability to Parliament.

28. There are other potential difficulties with an independent body. It would need to be widely accepted and seen as authoritative, a position that may not be quickly or easily achieved when it could be called upon to make appointments to politically controversial posts. If Ministers were taken out of the final selection process, it might diminish their ability to persuade people in senior positions in other walks of life to take on a substantial and often not well remunerated commitment.

29. In conclusion, we do not find the case for change proven. Some of the arguments for a wholly independent and impartial appointments system are persuasive, but there are practical difficulties which cannot be overcome at present. Accountability to Parliament is an important constitutional principle which we have no wish to weaken.

We recommend that ultimate responsibility for appointments should remain with Ministers.

30. Where a Minister has a conflict of interest—whether financial or because a close relative, friend or associate is among the leading candidates—it is axiomatic that the Minister in question should withdraw, and entrust the decision entirely to a Ministerial colleague. Although there is not such a clear conflict of interest where the relative, friend or associate of a Ministerial colleague is under consideration, we believe that Ministers should only make such appointments after taking advice from their Department's Permanent Secretary. We welcome the Government's willingness to issue clearer guidance to Ministers to ensure that reasons for appointment are fully set out and documented against the job specification in such cases. Such records could then be reviewed.

31. This leaves Ministers with considerable powers of patronage. It does not, however, follow that Ministers should act with unfettered discretion. The Government believes that "provided the safeguards are robust enough, the existing or proposed framework should be workable, responsive and effective". We broadly agree, although we do not believe that the existing or proposed safeguards are sufficiently robust. They need to be substantially improved, particularly in providing independent checks and balances. It is to those safeguards that we now turn.

Legal safeguards

32. When making appointments, Ministers must act within the law, which provides particular safeguards against discrimination on the grounds of gender or race. A Ministerial appointment can also be challenged on the grounds that the decision was ultra vires (ie. outside the Minister's legal powers) or perverse; or that the procedures did not accord with the rules of natural justice. The industrial tribunal or, in the case of judicial review, the courts, can require departments to disclose their procedures and reasoning and to justify them. It would, however, require considerable motivation for an individual to bring such an action and the circumstances in which it can be done are limited, so additional administrative safeguards are necessary.

Principles of selection

33. Perhaps the most fundamental safeguard is the establishment of clear published principles governing selection for appointment. The Government's evidence to us stated that:

> *"The Government is committed to the principle that selection for public appointments should be made on merit by the well-informed choice of individuals who through their qualifications, experience or qualities match the needs of the public body and the post in question"*

34. The competence of board members also has a direct bearing on standards of conduct. As the Audit Commission told us:

> *"Good leadership has a powerful influence. Conversely weakness in key appointments opens the way to abuse. Appointing someone who is not up to the job, however admirable they may be in other ways, is damaging"*

35. We support the Government's stated position.

We recommend that all public appointments should be governed by the overriding principle of appointment on merit.

36. This principle is deeply ingrained in British public life, but there remains some debate about how it should be applied. We now address two areas of concern to many of our witnesses, namely whether and how the political views of candidates should be taken into account, and the question of balance on boards of public bodies.

Political affiliation

37. There is no doubt that an effective board member of an executive NDPB or an NHS body must be committed to the achievement of the body's objectives. There was also widespread agreement, in the evidence we heard, that board members must be committed to working within the policy and resources framework set by the Minister. Appointed bodies should not be able to thwart or undermine the intentions of Ministers and Parliament. We agree with Archie Kirkwood MP that:

> *"...if you then found that you were putting people in charge of extremely important decision-making bodies which require a degree of leadership that are actually prepared openly to confront the political direction of the Government of the day, I think that makes the process of Government almost impossible to sustain. ..."*

38. We do not believe that this requires each board member to be personally committed to a particular policy, still less share the political thinking of a Minister. It is entirely possible to give dedicated service to a body out of a commitment to the public good, without necessarily supporting a particular policy direction or a particular way of organising a public service. Reasoned scepticism within the board may add to the quality of decision making and can sometimes be essential to protect the public interest.

39. There may be cases where the nature of a public body makes it important that individual political parties are represented on it. This Committee includes nominees of the Conservative, Labour and Liberal Democrat Parties. Specific provision was made in the National Lottery Act 1993 for the Leader of the Opposition to nominate a member of the Millenium Commission. Efforts are made when appointing Justices of the Peace to ensure that the political profile of the local bench reflects that of the community they serve.

40. These existing arrangements seem to work well, but we believe there are dangers in extending this approach more widely. Political activity might come to be seen as the route to positions in public service to the exclusion of people with no strong political views or of people with other relevant experience.

Balance

41. Except in limited circumstances such as those outlined above we do not believe that it is necessary or desirable to make political affiliation a criterion for appointment. It follows that we do not see any case for designating certain posts as "political" appointments which would be expected to be filled by a government supporter. Nor do we support the suggestion that there should be a general expectation of explicit political balance in appointments to executive NDPB and NHS bodies

42. We do, however, believe that the boards of public bodies should contain a balance of relevant skills, interests and backgrounds. This might include financial or legal skills or, for NHS bodies, clinical skills or other expertise in health issues. In NHS bodies, and some executive NDPBs, senior executives also sit on the board, and their attributes should also be taken into account in establishing a balanced board.

43. If the members are too similar in background and outlook there is unlikely to be the sort of healthy internal debate which is conducive to good decision making. As an Institute of Directors publication states, in relation to private sector companies, "it is after all the role of the non-executive to maintain an attitude of constructive scepticism[*]". A board which reflects the composition of the community it serves may also enjoy greater public confidence, thereby making the implementation of its work more effective.

> *"... the Association would like to see ... a broadening of the base from which* [NHS] *board members are drawn" (British Medical Association, written submission)*
>
> *"...one sees all over the country examples of health authorities and trust boards that are drawn from a wide base, including local councillors, business men, teachers, lawyers and others ..." (Alan Langlands, NHS Chief Executive).*
>
> *"...there is a general tendency for individuals to be appointed to more than one public body, once they have, so to speak, proved their credentials. This is a natural tendency ... but it is an unhealthy tendency too ... it tends to create a class of 'quangocrats' who may be chosen for their amenability and 'good behaviour' and to restrict the pluralism and diversity of talent on which a thriving appointments system should draw." (The Democratic Audit of Great Britain, written submission)*
>
> *"the facts do not suggest that quangos are packed with lookalikes" (Stanley Kalms, Chairman of Dixons plc, Chairman of a London health trust and member of the Funding Agency for Schools).*

44. It has been argued that the NDPB boards have become unbalanced, with appointments being made from a narrow circle of business and professional people. The answers to parliamentary questions asked by Alan Milburn MP showed that 152 out of 361

---

[*] 'The Non-executive Director', Institute of Directors, 1992.

chairs of NHS Trusts (ie. 42%) were current or retired company directors or business owners. John Monks, the General Secretary of the TUC, described this as "the cult of the businessman". This was contrasted with the decline in numbers of local authority members and trade unionists, and low representation of users or consumers. An associated concern, expressed by several of our witnesses, is that members of this narrow group are recruited to several different public bodies, creating a new class of "quangocrats"

45. Others argue that if there has been a shift in the balance towards greater representation of business, this is because business people have exactly the managerial and commercial skills that are required. It may also be a mistake to assume that business and professional people are a homogeneous group.

46. The extent to which boards are currently unbalanced is a matter of considerable debate, some of it highly political, and we find it difficult to draw any firm conclusions. Nonetheless we believe the principle is clear, and **we recommend that selection on merit should take account of the need to appoint boards which include a balance of skills and backgrounds. The basis on which members are appointed and how they are expected to fulfil their role should be explicit** (eg. whether members are any way representative of particular interests or viewpoints, or whether they are appointed purely as individuals). **The range of skills and background which are sought should be clearly specified**, normally as part of the job specifications prepared for particular posts, and should be sufficiently wide to promote healthy debate within the board.

Independent advice

47. At present advice to Ministers on appointments is provided by civil servants within departments (or within the NHS) often with the close involvement of the chairman and sometimes the chief executive of the body concerned. This is no different in essence to the way in which civil servants advise Ministers on other policy and operational issues. However, critics suggest that this can lead to such deliberations being conducted within a closed circle of advisers and, in particular, that Ministerial assumptions might often go unquestioned. Adding an independent element would increase the breadth and depth of the advice Ministers receive, and allow a range of community interests to be reflected in that advice. Public confidence would be enhanced if such advice included independent assurance that any proposed appointees had been scrutinised and found to be suitable for the post.

48. The Government is already implementing two major initiatives to include an element of independent advice in NHS appointments. A committee consisting of five independent members chaired by the Lord Provost of Edinburgh (an SNP Councillor), was established in 1994 by the Secretary of State for Scotland to advise him on NHS appointments in Scotland. In England, formal sifting panels are being introduced in each NHS Region with the option of including an independent member. Most of the 5,000 or so NHS appointments are therefore already covered by such arrangements, which do not appear to add significantly to the cost of the process. We believe that it would be both desirable and

cost-effective to extend the input of independent advice to the 4,000 posts in executive NDPBs (ie around 1,000 appointments per year). The appointment of Chairs, currently excluded from both NHS arrangements, should also be covered.

We recommend that all appointments to executive NDPBs or NHS bodies should be made after advice from a panel or committee which includes an independent element.

49. The committees or panels should be appointed by the relevant Secretary of State after wide consultation. It may often be appropriate for a body or bodies with major interests in the policy areas in question to be given rights of nomination. As a rule of thumb.

We recommend that each panel or committee should have at least one independent member and independent members should normally account for at least a third of membership.

Independence cannot be precisely defined but should normally mean that such a person has no operational role within the bodies or government departments concerned.

50. Some departments of state may find a single advisory committee sufficient. Panels covering particular areas may be needed for large numbers of recurring appointments. The Public Appointments Commissioner (see Paras 52–58 below) should advise on appropriate arrangements and approve them as part of each department's appointments system.

51. All candidates, regardless of how they are nominated, including those put forward by Ministers, should be scrutinised by a panel before being recommended for appointment. Ministers would not be obliged to accept the advisory committee's recommendations, but if they intend to appoint someone not approved by the panel or committee as suitable for the post, they would be obliged to inform the Public Appointments Commissioner publicly.

Monitoring and Scrutiny

52. The main weakness both in the current arrangements and in those proposed in the PAU review is the absence of effective external scrutiny. Select Committees can of course examine departments' public appointments in the same way as any other aspect of government activity, but in practice they lack the tools to do this in detail and they have many other priorities. The Public Appointments Unit appears to have little role in monitoring the working of its central guidance beyond that necessary to produce its annual report, which is largely a statistical summary of appointments. Indeed, the recent review found that, in practice, the way appointments were made varied considerably across departments. There is no mechanism for the regular review of the work of individual departments and no means of identifying failures of system or practice.

53. We believe that an independent body is needed to undertake the continued standard-setting and monitoring that will enhance and sustain public confidence in the appointments process. The PAU review recommended that compliance should be

monitored every five years through departments' normal internal audit procedures. This would be useful, but we believe that an external monitoring regime would act as a more effective discipline on departments and command greater public confidence. A more specialised approach focusing specifically on appointments is likely to be more effective.

We therefore recommend that a new independent Commissioner for Public Appointments should be appointed, who may be one of the Civil Service Commissioners.

54.   The Commissioner's role would be analogous in many respects to that of the First Civil Service Commissioner. In view of these similarities, and to give the post-holder ready access to a body of relevant expertise and experience, it may be advantageous for them to be linked in organisational terms.

"We believe that changes in the appointments arrangements [for the NHS] *are desirable to make them more robust, open and transparent; and this includes an independent element. They will thus have the confidence of local communities" (Chris Robinson, Chairman of the National Association of Health Authorities and Trusts)*

"I think that if the best practices of public appointments and advertising, with a body such as the Civil Service Commission overseeing the probity of it, were extended to Quangoland, a lot of the problem would evaporate …" (Dr Peter Hennessy, Professor of Contemporary British History, Queen Mary and Westfield College, University of London).

"… it is a truism that politicians are not widely accorded a great deal of trust… and it is sometimes helpful to have an outside body, as a seal of approval if nothing else, which the public can have a degree of confidence in…" (David Heath, Leader of the Liberal Democrat group , Association of County Councils).

"… in the final event, after we had interviewed various candidates, the nominations were in the hands of the Secretary of State and we don't quite know exactly at the end of the day how he made his final choice… " (Robert Gunn, Chairman of the Further Education Funding Council, on the appointment of council members)

"Obscure appointments processes are intrinsically unfair to those in our community who have skills to offer but are unaware of the opportunities to offer and employ those skills. They also breed suspicions which undermine the credibility of the boards concerned…" (Stevenage Borough Council, written submission)

---

55.   The Commissioner's responsibilities should include all public appointments to executive NDPBs, including NHS bodies. This work would mirror the approach now taken by Civil Service Commissioners, in that systematic sample auditing of departmental procedures for public appointments would be conducted rather than detailed monitoring

of individual recruitment exercises. The Commissioner should also have the right to initiate investigations whether of certain types of appointment; of a particular department's programme; or of individual appointments. The Commissioner should have the same power to require departments to provide information about all stages of the appointments including selection by Ministers. Taken as whole, this should allow regulation to be undertaken with a light touch, and without introducing unnecessary bureaucracy.

We recommend that the Public Appointments Commissioner should monitor, regulate and approve departmental appointments procedures.

56. One of the first tasks of the new Commissioner should be to produce up-to-date guidance taking into account the PAU Review, this Committee's report and the government's response to it. Thereafter the Commissioner should monitor the operations of this central guidance, update it as necessary, and report on its operation in practice. The Commissioner should seek to keep abreast of best practice in the public and private sectors, and promulgate such practice to Departments. The Commissioner would also approve departments' own procedures and guidance.

We recommend that the Public Appointments Commissioner should publish an annual report on the operation of the public appointments system, including statistical information of the type published at present.

57. The Commissioner will need an administrative arm, and **we recommend that the Public Appointments Unit should be taken out of the Cabinet Office and placed under the control of the Public Appointments Commissioner.** It should maintain all its existing functions, but its remit and resources should be enhanced as necessary to allow it to fulfil the new functions of the Public Appointments Commissioner.

58. We comment elsewhere that legislation is being considered to bring the Civil Service under statute rather than prerogative. It may be appropriate in due course for the arrangements for the Public Appointments Commissioner to be put on a statutory footing, but we do not believe that it is necessary to wait for legislation to make the necessary administrative arrangements.

Openness

59. Some of the major concerns about appointments focus on openness (providing information about appointments) and transparency (making it clear what the appointment process is and how it works). We have heard concerns that, in many cases, it is unclear how names are gathered for consideration, what criteria these names are considered against and how the person appointed is chosen. Critics say that a widespread perception of secrecy has undermined public confidence.

60. We welcome the emphasis in the PAU review on documenting at the outset of the process a job description, a specification of the qualities sought in candidates and a description of the appointments procedures to be followed. We believe this information should be available to all candidates and members of the public. We support the PAU's recommendations for appointments to be announced publicly and for lists of people appointed to be available both centrally and locally.

61. We also welcome the presumption in favour of advertising posts, backed up where appropriate with executive search. We note that following a major Scottish Office campaign in 1992, of advertising and seeking nominations from interested organisations, 58% of subsequent NHS appointments came from these sources. This does not mean that all posts will be filled with candidates found through advertising. Other channels must remain open for directly approaching candidates, who may not previously have considered lending their talents to the public service. For the appointment of senior people to major national bodies it will remain important not to subject them to an overly bureaucratic process.

62. **We recommend that all Secretaries of State should report annually on the public appointments made by their departments.** This would supplement the Public Appointments Commissioner's annual report by providing a more detailed breakdown of appointments or classes of appointments, and would describe any major changes to the departmental procedures agreed with the Commissioner. It could form part of the department's annual report or be a free-standing document.

63. We recognise, however, that there is a balance to be struck between openness and the privacy of individuals. The procedures should be as transparent as possible, but we do not believe that information about individuals should be placed in the public domain until such time as they are appointed and can therefore be said to have entered public life. Databases of those who have applied or indicated their willingness to serve should remain confidential, as should any discussions of individual candidates and advice to Ministers. To put such discussions on the public record could inhibit those advising Ministers from being frank and deter some candidates from putting themselves forward. We believe the Public Appointments Commissioner will be a sufficient safeguard to ensure that procedures are operated as intended.

Declarations of political affiliation

64. This balance is particularly difficult to strike where the political inclinations of candidates are concerned. The PAU review deals adequately with identifying the potential conflicts of interest which candidates may experience on appointment, including those arising from appointments to several public bodies. However, they looked to us for guidance on whether candidates should be required to declare their political interests.

65. It is said that without such information to hand, Ministers are better able to make appointments untainted by party political considerations. We find this argument unconvincing. With 10,000 appointments to make each year it is unlikely that Ministers would routinely seek out such information, but many candidates for the most important appointments will have known political affiliations, of which Ministers will be aware.

66. There are considerable difficulties with requiring any declarations of political affiliation or experience to be made. It could be regarded as an unfair intrusion into people's privacy; it could act as a deterrent to people applying; and it could wrongly imply that decisions made on merit were influenced by politics. However, on balance, we believe the drawbacks are outweighed by the benefit to the public interest.

67. At present, the PAU's standard application form does not specifically ask about political affiliation, but where details of a person's political experience (eg as an officer of the local party) are offered, these are held on file. If this information were required as standard it could be used by the Public Appointments Commissioner to monitor the success rates of candidates of different political persuasions. If the results of this monitoring were then to be published it could act as a discipline against abuse as well as helping to restore public confidence in the system.

68. There is a wide spectrum of party commitment. We agree with the PAU review that inclination to vote and membership of a party should remain private matters. But by taking office within a party, writing or speaking publicly on party political issues or standing as a candidate for election as a local councillor or MP a person might be considered to have made their political allegiance a matter of public record. It would not, therefore, be unreasonable for that public declaration to be restated when they apply or are considered for a public appointment. It should not, however, be assumed that such activities in the past imply a current belief or level of activity, and any requirement to declare must include a time limit.

We recommend that candidates should be required to declare any significant political activity (including office-holding, public speaking and candidature for election) which they have undertaken in the last five years.

69. The declaration would not be made public until the candidate was appointed when it would be entered on the body's register of interests. However, the Public Appointments Commissioner would be able to monitor the political balance of candidates and appointees.

The appointments process: a code of practice & "proportionality"

70. We have received a considerable volume of evidence highlighting the best practice in appointments procedures and making suggestions for improving the current system. Indeed, much of this has come from the Government, based on the PAU review. Based on this evidence and our conclusions on the key issues discussed above, we have drawn up a draft code of practice for the procedures which should be used for making appointments to executive NDPBs and NHS bodies. We believe the code works with the grain of existing good practice and provides a practical standard for departments to meet. It will help departments to adopt a more consistent approach, thus promoting not only the maintenance of high standards, but also greater understanding of the process among candidates and the general public.

71. The PAU review stresses that appointments procedures need to be subject to the principle of "proportionality". This means that a process which may be right and cost-effective for a full-time, highly paid post responsible for significant public spending is unlikely to be necessary for a part-time, one day a month, unpaid appointment to an advisory committee. We accept this principle, providing that it is applied with some rigour and does not become an easy excuse for bureaucratic convenience. The test of proportionality should be tightly drawn, with the reasons for all derogations from the code of practice clearly documented and capable of review by the Public Appointments

Draft Code of Practice for Public Appointments procedures

Defining the task (job description) and the qualities sought ("person specification");

- Job descriptions and a summary of the key qualities sought ("a person specification") should always be documented, be publicly available, be sent to all candidates and be held for scrutiny by the Public Appointments Commissioner.

- A description of the appointments process should be similarly documented and made available.

Identifying a field of candidates

- A wide field of candidates should be obtained by making appropriate use of:
  - Advertising—both general and for individual posts;
  - Executive search;
  - Consultation with interested bodies, which should always include any recognised consultative/user groups and, for local appointments, the elected local authorities;
  - Maintaining and using databases of interested and appropriate people.

- It should always be possible for anyone to nominate anyone, including themselves, and this should be made clear in all advertising and publicity.

Selecting a short list, and recommending candidates to Ministers

- The sifting of candidates should be undertaken or overseen by committees or panels with independent members.

- Any candidate recommended to Ministers should have been approved as suitable for the post by the committee or panel, taking up references where appropriate.

Choosing the preferred candidate(s)

- Appointments should be made on the basis of merit, with the aim of achieving a balance of relevant skills and backgrounds on the board.

- Candidates should not normally be appointed without having been interviewed either by the advisory committee/panel or, in the case of more senior appointments, by Ministers or senior officials.

- Re-appointments should not be automatic. The performance of the post-holder should be reviewed.

Confirming the appointment

- All appointments should be announced through press notices and other suitable means—either individually or for minor appointments in batches at least quarterly; and departments should report annually on their procedures.

- Sponsor departments and individual NDPBs & NHS bodies should hold lists of their members which outline who they are and when their term expires.

Commissioner. The amount of public expenditure, the importance of the public functions and the degree of power or influence exercised by the public body should be the primary reference point, rather than the remuneration or hours of the post.

72. Finalising the code of practice and the approach to "proportionality" should, however, depend on the ease with which they can be overseen by the new Commissioner. **We recommend, therefore, that the Public Appointments Commissioner should draw up a code of practice for public appointments procedures.** This would be undertaken as part of the revision of central guidance on appointments. **Reasons for departures from this code on grounds of proportionality should be documented and capable of review.** The Commissioner may draw up a working definition of "proportionality" to guide departments.

Propriety

73. We now turn to standards of conduct in quangos and how to ensure the highest standards of propriety. We take propriety to encompass not only financial rectitude, but a sense of the values and behaviour appropriate to the public sector.

> *Public bodies and their Boards must at all times observe the highest standards of impartiality, integrity and objectivity in relation to the stewardship of public funds and management of the bodies concerned. (Code of Best Practice for Board Members of Public Bodies, HM Treasury, 1994)*
>
> *We understand 'good conduct' for members and employees of public bodies to be a person's responsibility to act fairly and in good faith, and in a disinterested way to meet the specified objectives of the body to which he or she has been appointed or elected. (The Chartered Institute for Public Finance and Accountancy (CIPFA), written submission)*

74. The available evidence suggests that, in general, the board members of executive NDPBs and NHS bodies are committed to the principles and values of public service and perform their duties to high standards of integrity. The Audit Commission told us, for example, that:

> *"The vast majority of people in local government and the NHS behave honestly and make proper use of public funds. Most people show a strong commitment to public service".*

However, some lapses from these high standards have been recorded. Some cases have attracted considerable publicity, and public unease has grown. A number of such cases are reviewed in the Public Accounts Committee's report on 'The Proper Conduct of Public Business' (8th Report, 1993/94 session).

75. Nothing we recommend can guarantee high standards of propriety. Human weakness will always be with us; mistakes will always be made; and the corrupt will always seek new ways to play the system. But appropriate safeguards minimise the risk of such impropriety occuring or remaining undetected. They include clear expectations of standards of individual behaviour; appropriate internal controls to provide checks and balances against individual misconduct; and external supervision to hold the organisation accountable. Above all, such safeguards help to create a climate and culture in which high standards of propriety are valued.

The need for review

76. Our approach has been to compare the safeguards employed by executive NDPBs and NHS bodies with benchmarks of good practice from elsewhere, particularly from central and local government. We recognise that there are important differences between branches of the public service in their purpose, their traditions and in the way in which they are accountable to the public. However, we are more impressed by the similarities than the differences—they all perform public functions with public money, and the public expectation of high standards is essentially the same.

77. We therefore agree in principle with the Audit Commission and several other witnesses that there should be a presumption in favour of using the most rigorous safeguards more consistently across the public sector. While not all practices can be simply transferred from one context to another, variation from the best practice should be based on a conscious choice, capable of being justified in public.

> *"… where local government rules are more rigorous, or where sanctions are stronger, there should be a presumption in favour of extending the same principles. …the onus should be on those who oppose such measures to show why they are inappropriate. Equally, …where the NHS and other bodies have stronger requirements, there should be a presumption in favour of extending those requirements into local government." (The Audit Commission, written evidence)*
>
> *"Our view is that the same standards should operate across the public sector, and we would not oppose the imposition of the possibility of surcharge in the case of NHS boards." (Chris Robinson, Chairman of the National Association of Health Authorities and Trusts)*

78. Although it is not easy to draw effective comparisons across a wide range of different organisations, a clear overall pattern emerges from the evidence we received. As we note in Chapter 3, the new Civil Service Code will supplement an ample body of long-established and often mandatory codes and conventions covering central government. Local authorities have an extensive statutory framework of safeguards, which has been updated considerably since the Poulson scandal in the 1970s. By contrast, although there is comprehensive central guidance for NDPBs, it seems to be interpreted very flexibly and is underpinned by an ad hoc collection of individual statutes.

79. Following some well publicised shortcomings in certain NDPBs and parts of the NHS, the government has made significant efforts to tighten up these safeguards. Best practice among NDPBs and NHS bodies certainly compares well with the rest of the public sector. However, the variety of practice still opens up real potential for impropriety, and fuels a public perception that standards are not rigorously upheld.

80. To take just one example, failure to declare a conflict of interest, or to withdraw from a relevant discussion, has for some years been a criminal offence for a local councillor. It is only in the last year or so that taking part in business where a conflict of interest exists has been addressed in NDPB and NHS codes of conduct, and even now no penalties are laid down in respect of breaches. Local councillors are subject to surcharge and disqualification, while no quango board members can be surcharged and only some are liable to the threat of disqualification. We examine later how the arrangements for external scrutiny by auditors and Ombudsmen vary.

81. In the following pages we identify some key safeguards which should be applied on a more uniform basis. Given the relatively short time scale available for our first report and also the diversity of the bodies we are considering, we have attempted to focus on principles rather than detail. This report should be seen as an initial stage in the process.

We recommend that a review be undertaken by the Government with a view to producing a more consistent legal framework governing propriety and accountability in public bodies, including executive NDPBs, NHS bodies and local government. This should involve all relevant departments and be co-ordinated by the Cabinet Office and the Treasury.

83. We now focus our substantive recommendations in three areas which reflect the key principles outlined in our introduction. They are:

    i)   Codes of Conduct: ensuring a clear framework for corporate & individual standards;

    ii) Scrutiny: establishing effective procedures—both internal & external—for monitoring & enforcing such standards; and improving public confidence in quangos by increasing the transparency of their actions

    iii) Training: ensuring that both board members & staff are fully aware of the standards expected, particularly through better induction training.

Codes of Conduct

83. The gravest concerns about standards of propriety focus on the misuse of public office to pursue personal interest. Directing contracts, business or expenditure towards organisations with which members or staff have a personal or financial connection is a particularly acute and widespread concern.

84. Sometimes deliberate fraud or corruption is involved and this can be dealt with through the law, although administrative action can have a crucial preventative role. However, impropriety can also arise out of ignorance of the rules, uncertainty about what the rules are, or a desire to get things done quickly even if it means bending rules or cutting corners*.

85. Non-executives from outside the public sector may lack experience in the disciplines involved in the handling of public money. In the NHS, for example, a recent survey of 2,600 board members by the NHS Management Executive found that around half of them felt it permissable to sign contracts first and get approval afterwards (49 per cent), or to break the rules "if it was in the NHS's interests" (46 per cent). That is not to say that the private sector lacks ethics or values, although they may differ in some respects from the traditions of the public sector. Chris Robinson of NAHAT felt that problems had arisen in the NHS because of "the inevitable tension, between the public service ethos and the adoption of a market-orientated health service". At best this can be a healthy and creative tension, but it can also create the potential for ethical ambiguity to develop affecting both board members and staff.

86. Such uncertainties may be compounded if internal procedures and controls are weak, or are disrupted at times of major organisational change. We heard that some cases of impropriety may actually have resulted from a mistaken understanding by public servants of the supposed freedoms that greater commercialisation would bring. Clear expectations of standards of conduct are important for public servants at all levels. Non-executive board members have an important role to play, both in guiding and controlling the executive management, but also in being prepared to challenge the chair and fellow directors.

87. Much has recently been done to improve and standardise arrangements to secure high standards of conduct in NDPBs and NHS bodies. The Treasury and the Cabinet Office produce two key documents to guide Departments and NDPBs. 'Non-departmental public bodies: A Guide for Departments' covers all aspects of quangos including their creation, management, financing, accountability, review and abolition. It was last issued in 1992, and is currently being updated.

88. The most important recent development is the Treasury's 'Code of Best Practice for Board Members of Public Bodies' issued in June 1994. It is intended as a model which public bodies should implement with any modifications which may be necessary to take account of their own particular characteristics and circumstances. It is based on the principles set out in the Cadbury report's Code of Best Practice[†], suitably adapted for the particular circumstances of the public sector. A similar NHS Code of Conduct/Code of Accountability took effect in England in April 1994, with very similar codes also being issued to NHS bodies in Scotland. Equivalent documents but in a different form were issued in Wales in January 1995.

89. Such codes are an increasingly accepted part of business practice. Professor Jack Mahoney[‡] told us that between a quarter and a third of major companies now have such codes and the Institute of Business Ethics estimated that this was likely to rise to one in

---

* The Audit Commission's written evidence includes these amongst the main reasons for improper actions.

† 'Report of the Committee on the Financial Aspects of Corporate Governance: the Code of Best Practice', December 1992.

‡ The Professor of Business Ethics and Social Responsibility at London Business School.

two in the near future. Local councillors are covered by a statutory code of conduct, while the local authority associations have developed a code for officers. Many NDPBs have already developed their own Codes based on the Treasury model.

90. This approach is preferable to developing extra layers of controls. As the Audit Commission say:

> *"Bureaucracy and overburdensome rules will not ensure good conduct. At their worst such devices not only stifle initiative, but may lead to improper behaviour."*

91. It has been suggested that a common code ought to apply throughout the public sector. We would agree that there are certain core principles such as those we outlined in Chapter 1, but we found persuasive the arguments of the Institute of Business Ethics and others in support of more specific codes tailored to each body. The process of drawing up such codes allows each body to conduct a detailed consideration of particular issues of conduct which arise in their operations, and encourages compliance by developing a sense of "ownership".

We recommend that the adoption of a code of conduct for board members should be made mandatory for each executive NDPB and NHS body. The code should be agreed with the sponsor department who should ensure that it meets the principles of the Treasury code.

It should be mandatory for the board of each executive NDPB and NHS body to adopt a code of conduct for their staff. The Cabinet Office (OPSS) may wish to consider preparing and maintaining a model code for NDPBs to adopt or adapt to their own circumstances. All Codes should be public documents, freely and easily available.

Content of Codes

92. We believe that the codes of conduct for board members and their staff should be as rigorous as those which apply to Ministers and civil servants. We do not wish to comment in detail on the content of such codes. The Cadbury report, the Treasury code, and the many specific codes which have already been developed cover this ground thoroughly. However, certain key principles stand out in the evidence we received. Codes of Conduct need to embrace both the individual responsibilities of board members and staff to uphold high standards of personal behaviour, and the collective responsibility of board members, in particular, to ensure good corporate governance. As the Audit Commission told us "how people behave when holding public office reflects their individual moral character and principles, but it is also influenced by the institutional structures in which they work". Some organisations have chosen to separate these subjects into complementary codes.

93. Standards of individual behaviour need to include, especially, the clear expectation that public servants should at all times act in the public interest and should resolve any conflicts that may arise with their personal interests. Board members should be required to enter relevant interests in a public register, to declare any interests which arise during the course of business and to withdraw where appropriate from discussions or decisions. In cases of doubt the presumption should be in favour of declaring and withdrawing. The rules on

gifts and hospitality should be just as clear and should be no less stringent than those which apply in the Civil Service. The arrangements for staff will depend on the work they undertake but the rules should be particularly tight for staff with responsibility for purchasing, or awarding contracts. It is important that board members and staff are made aware of these expectations and periodically reminded of them (see our comments on training at paras 124–126).

94. Effective corporate governance should include checks and balances at a senior level so that no individual enjoys unfettered discretion; systems of management and financial control; an internal audit function and an audit committee; and a formal scheme of delegation of authority, including a schedule of decisions which are reserved to the board. In the remainder of this chapter, we consider how key aspects of internal controls, external supervision and openness can be strengthened.

Enforcement of Codes

95. Codes of conduct should be binding.

We recommend that, as with the NHS codes, board members and staff should be required on appointment to undertake to uphold and abide by the relevant code, and compliance should be a condition of appointment.

96. At present there often seem to be no clear mechanisms for identifying whether codes are being complied with or for imposing sanctions where they are not. In theory, non-executive board members can be dismissed by Ministers, but it is not clear in what circumstances this penalty would be used or whether other penalties might be considered appropriate for lesser offences.

We recommend that sponsor departments should develop clear disciplinary procedures for board members of executive NDPBs and NHS bodies with appropriate penalties for failing to observe codes of conduct.

In time, these procedures should take account of the review of the legal framework for issues of propriety which we recommend in para 81.

Scrutiny

97. In a democratic society it is important that the actions of those in public office should be subject to scrutiny by the representatives of the people. Parliament is at the heart of this, but a variety of intermediary bodies and other administrative procedures have been developed to assist it. Here we use the term scrutiny in a broad sense to include internal checks, external supervision and direct scrutiny by the public through greater openness.

Internal controls: a designated officer for propriety issues?

98. In executive NDPBs, the boards' responsibilities for financial control are supported by a designated accounting officer, but there is no equivalent support on propriety in general as there is, for example, in local authorities.

99.   For most executive NDPBs the sponsor department designates the senior full-time official (the Chief Executive or equivalent) as the NDPB accounting officer, responsible to Parliament for all resources under his or her control and for signing the accounts. Central guidance for NDPB accounting officers was last revised in December 1994. The NHS Chief Executive currently acts as accounting officer for the whole NHS, including health authorities and trusts. Proposals are being considered to delegate some functions to a more local level so that Chief Executives in health authorities and trusts also become formally accountable. They can already be called before Parliamentary Select Committees.

100.   Local authorities have three officers with individual statutory responsibilities. The Head of Paid Service is responsible for personnel matters. The Chief Finance Officer has responsibilities for financial probity, auditing and production of accounts which are broadly analogous to those of an NDPB accounting officer. In addition, the Local Government and Housing Act 1989 requires every local authority to appoint a "monitoring officer", who is required to report to the authority on any breach of any statute or of any statutory code of practice by a council, a committee or an officer of the council. The monitoring officer is also required to make a report in any case of maladministration or injustice.

"None of us is so perfect that we can rely on ourselves to put our own houses in order at all times and in all events. As a club we tend to see things from within the club" (Geoffrey Filkin, Secretary of the Association of District Councils)

"It is apparent that guidelines where matters are left to the judgement of individuals are not effective" (David Veness, Assistant Commissioner, Metropolitan Police)

"We believe that wherever public money is spent in any significant quantity, then the principles of public audit ought to apply. By the principles of public audit we mean: that external auditors should be independently appointed and be independent of the body under audit; that the audit should comprise not only a probity audit which ensures that money is honestly and properly spent, but that there should be a value for money element … ; Then, finally that auditors should be entitled to publish reports in the public interest wherever they feel that it is important that the public understands where misappropriation or misuse of funds has taken place. These reports in the public interest are a very important check and balance to ensure that high standards of public life are maintained." (Sir David Cooksey, Chairman of the Audit Commission).

"Rules alone do not prevent malpractice, public scrutiny does" (Keith Henshall, Institute of Public Relations)

---

101.   Some private sector companies have a compliance officer with some of these responsibilities, while in others a similar role is fulfilled by the company secretary. The submission we received from the National Association of Health Authorities and Trusts (NAHAT) advocated that NHS boards should have the equivalent of a company secretary,

whose role would include some duties similar to those of a monitoring officer. We believe that designating an individual officer would help to maintain a commitment to propriety within the NDPB or NHS body and would improve accountability and scrutiny.

102.   We have considered whether this office should be separate from the accounting officer function. This would help to reduce the risk, particularly in smaller public bodies, of a chairman and chief executive overstepping the bounds of propriety in pursuing some particular project. On the other hand, there would be considerable overlap with the role of the accounting officer for ensuring financial probity, and there is a danger that clear lines of accountability through the chief executive and board could become blurred.

We recommend that the role of executive NDPB and NHS accounting officers should be redefined to emphasise their formal responsibility for all aspects of propriety.

103.   If a body does not have a formally designated accounting officer, as with health authorities and NHS trusts, an equivalent officer should be designated to fulfil this role. The designated officer should advise the board as a whole on any actions or proposed actions which would be contrary to any statute or code of practice, including the code of conduct for board members; and should have a duty to inform the sponsor department if this advice is disregarded. This would complement the existing duty of accounting officers throughout the public service to notify the public auditors if a public body incurs or proposes to incur expenditure which is illegal.

External audit

104.   Regular audit is an important way of uncovering irregularities in financial matters—whether they are due to outright fraud and corruption or result from laxity in following proper procedures—and of establishing public confidence that public money is being properly spent. For executive NDPBs, the Comptroller & Auditor General (C&AG) is either the statutory auditor, with the work being undertaken by the National Audit Office (NAO) or a major accountancy firm, or has inspection rights either on a statutory basis or by agreement. The public auditor for NHS bodies is the Audit Commission, which uses the district audit service or major accountancy firms, and which performs the same function for local authorities.

105.   There are differences in these audit regimes, and there may be scope for bringing them all up to the standard of the best. The Audit Commission has more limited powers in respect of the NHS than in respect of local authorities. It does not, for example, have the power to publish reports directly where it believes this to be in the public interest. Last year, the Commission published fifteen public interest reports on local government and submitted three reports on NHS bodies to Ministers, who decide whether to publish. The Audit Commission told us that Ministers have been very open about publishing these reports, although the Chief Executive of the NHS conceded that they do not always come into the public view. The C&AG's findings are subject to public scrutiny as he reports directly to Parliament and works closely with the Public Accounts Committee. Although we

recognise that this difference reflects lines of accountability where NHS bodies are accountable in the first instance to the relevant Secretary of State, the absence of automatic public scrutiny does seem to us to represent an anomaly.

We recommend that the Audit Commission should be authorised to publish public interest reports on NHS bodies at its own discretion. This would be consistent with moves towards greater openness which we discuss later.

106.   There are other differences, and while some are relatively minor, others are more significant. In particular, the public auditors have a power to apply to the courts to surcharge individual members and officers of local authorities but not those of NHS bodies or NDPBs. There may be good reasons for maintaining differences in the audit regimes for different public bodies, but the current variation seems to be the result of the introduction of measures on an ad hoc basis. The C&AG also told us that he could see little logic in the way in which he was appointed as the auditor for some NDPBs but only had inspection rights for others. In addition some of these inspection rights are set out in the statutes which create or govern the NDPB but others have to be negotiated with the sponsor department, taking up resources which could be better employed elsewhere.

107.   We believe, in principle, that the propriety of all public expenditure should be capable of review by the appropriate public auditing body. We see much merit in the Comptroller and Auditor General being granted inspection rights over all public expenditure. Where such rights do not already exist, this could be achieved through contract terms or grant conditions attached to public funding. Care would be needed to ensure that no unnecessary bureaucracy would be introduced and, in particular, that duplication of effort by different auditors would be minimised.

108.   We are not here recommending an extension of the NAO's role as auditor. The existence of two bodies supervising the audit of different public bodies provides a valuable creative tension which can only serve to raise standards. For the same reason and to ensure that the auditors themselves are under pressure to perform well, we believe that private firms should be able to compete for appointment as auditors of public bodies, and that auditors should be changed at regular (at most five yearly) intervals.

109.   This is a complex and technical field, and we believe that the remaining anomalies need to be tackled in a systematic way.

We recommend that the Treasury review the arrangements for external audit of public bodies, with a view to applying the best practices to all.

Dealing with complaints

110.   Since 1967, the external review of public complaints by an independent Ombudsman has become a recognised and respected part of public administration. Individual citizens may lodge complaints if they believe they have experienced injustice as a result of maladministration. Not all such cases will be the result of impropriety—often poor procedures, inefficiency or mistakes are to blame—but it is an important check on the improper use of public office. The existence of an external check is a powerful discipline on public bodies to resolve complaints in the first place.

111.   NHS bodies are all subject to the jurisdiction of the Health Services Ombudsman. Legislation* lists the NDPBs which are subject to the jurisdiction of the Parliamentary Commissioner for Administration (PCA)—the central government Ombudsman. Most of the major executive NDPBs are included, but some are not. Many of those excluded have little or no direct dealings with the public, yet if their functions were part of local or central government (including executive agencies) they would automatically fall within jurisdiction. The Parliamentary Select Committee on the PCA has recommended that the legislation be amended to specify those bodies which are included rather then excluded from the PCA's jurisdiction. The Government has undertaken to look carefully at this proposal, and we believe it would represent a welcome clarification if a practical way can be found to implement it.

"Whistleblowing"

112.   One of the conditions which can lead to an environment in which fraud and malpractice can occur, according to the Metropolitan Police, is the absence of a mechanism by which concerns can be brought to light without jeopardising the informant[†]. The Audit Commission figures (see Table 3) show that information from staff is a major contribution to the detection of fraud and corruption in the NHS. Concerned staff were instrumental in uncovering serious irregularities at two colleges of further education[‡]. As Public Concern at Work, a leading charity in this field, told us in their submission, "if there is a breach of the standards appropriate in a public body it is likely that the first people to suspect it will be the staff who work there"

Table 3: Method of detection of proven fraud and corruption in the NHS, over 3 years to 1994.

Information from staff	22%
Information from patients	9%
Accidental	8%
Internal controls	22%
Internal audit	18%
External audit	10%
Other	11%

Source: Audit Commission, in *'Protecting the Public Purse 2: Ensuring Probity in the NHS'*, 1994

113.   However, it seems that staff concerns come to light despite rather than because of the system. We are not aware of any central guidance for executive NDPBs, and whilst the NHS have issued comprehensive central guidance[§], the Audit Commission's 1994 report found that none of the 17 NHS bodies they visited had a well-publicised system which informed staff whom they should contact if they suspect fraud and corruption.

---

*   Schedule 2 of the Parliamentary and Health Commissioners Act 1987 (as amended from time to time, particularly when new NDPBs are created).
†   Metropolitan Police, Fraud Squad, Public Sector Corruption Unit, written evidence.
‡   As described to us by the Chairman and Chief Executive of the Further Education Funding Council.
§   Guidance for staff on relations with the public and the media, issued by the NHS Management Executive, June 1993.

114.   There is public concern about "gagging clauses" in public employees' contracts of employment, which prevent them from speaking out to raise concerns about standards of propriety. Where a loyal employee has concerns about impropriety, making public allegations in the media is unlikely to be their first recourse. However, without some way of voicing their concern, and without some confidence that it will be taken seriously and dealt with if necessary, they may feel they have no other option. We agree with the sentiment expressed by Robert Sheldon MP, Chairman of the Public Accounts Committee that "public money must never be allowed to have silence clauses". On the other hand, we would not wish to encourage vexatious or irresponsible complaints which undermine public confidence in institutions without due cause. We believe the best way to achieve this balance is to develop sound internal procedures backed by an external review.

115.   Non-executives often see themselves as a safeguard against such problems but staff may be suspicious or reluctant to approach them. The Audit Commission found a third of the NHS staff they interviewed would take no action in the face of impropriety because of fears of losing their jobs if they 'rock the boat'. Alan Langlands, the Chief Executive of the NHS, recognised that, "a sustained effort is required to ensure that these guidelines are properly carried through, both in spirit and in detail at local level". As Public Concern at Work point out, "although the employee is well placed to sound the alarm, he or she has most to lose by raising the matter".

116.   In Chapter 3, we propose that each government department and agency nominate an officer to provide a clear route for staff concerns about improper conduct. This will be supported by a further route of appeal to the Civil Service Commissioners. The NHS guidance suggests that NHS bodies might wish to designate such an officer.

We recommend that each executive NDPB and NHS body that has not already done so should nominate an official or board member entrusted with the duty of investigating staff concerns about propriety raised confidentially. Staff should be able to make complaints without going through the normal management structure, and should be guaranteed anonymity. If they remain unsatisfied, staff should also have a clear route for raising concerns about issues of propriety with the sponsor department.

Openness

117.   Public concern has in many cases been magnified by a perception of excessive secrecy in quangos. Submissions we received highlighted the refusal of some public bodies to provide information even where it had previously been in the public domain; the excessive use of commercial confidentiality to justify withholding information; and difficulty in finding where information could be obtained. Greater openness can only make impropriety more difficult to hide, and therefore more hazardous to perpetrate.

118.   Some witnesses, including the local authority associations, suggested that NDPBs and NHS bodies should be subject to statutory provisions such as those which apply to local government. These ensure, in particular, that all papers put before the council or any

of its committees are public documents. On the other hand, a common statutory framework might be too inflexible to apply to a wide range of public bodies performing very different functions. We believe that more experience in operating the Government's openness code is required before further major changes are considered.

"Public scrutiny of what people do is probably the most powerful pressure towards probity of conduct" (The Audit Commission, written evidence)

"The general rule for the conduct of NDPBs should be transparency except in cases of commercial or personal confidentiality. Minutes of decisions taken should be available to the public" (Demos, written evidence)

"At a local level, quangos affect crucial areas of people's lives. Local editors... say that there is a growing feeling that people are alienated and feel powerless to influence the decision making of such bodies ... One of the reasons is the secrecy with which quangos are shrouded.
(Santha Rasaiah, Parliamentary and Legal Committee, Guild of Editors)

"... the public are not only consumers of, but shareholders in public services. They should expect standards of disclosure and accountability no less than shareholders would have in respect of the board of a commercial organisation. At the moment these fall a long way short. ..."
(Anne Caldwell, correspondent)

---

119.   The Government's Code of Practice on Access to Government Information published in 1994 applies to those NDPBs which are subject to the jurisdiction of the Ombudsman, who handles any complaints about its application. Cabinet Office guidance requires the same principles to be applied to other executive NDPBs. The NHS has also issued a 'Code of Practice on Openness in the NHS', which as well as these general principles sets out mandatory requirements and good practice for each of the main NHS organisations.

120.   There are many examples of good practice in NDPBs and NHS bodies. We have consolidated the best features of these codes into a standard of best practice for openness. We recognise that not all of these practices can be applied to every public body. Public bodies should seek to be as open with the public as is consistent with good administration, but there needs to be some flexibility about how this principle is applied in different circumstances. There are three broad points arising from the standard of best practice that we would like to emphasise.

121.   On access to information, we believe attention needs to be given to ensuring that members of the public are aware of these codes of openness, and can understand what information they have the right to see; what information they do not; and why.

122.   On meetings, we recognise the danger that full and frank discussion of difficult issues could be inhibited if members of the public are admitted to meetings. The result would be less transparency since real debate would be driven into internal executive

structures. We do not therefore recommend requiring all board meetings to be open to the public, although where a public body chose to do this we would welcome it. We note that a recent survey by the NHS Trust Federation showed that more than half of trusts held more than one public meeting each year (the statutory minimum) and five trusts held all their meetings in public.

123.   Finally, we believe that publishing key information makes it easier for the public to obtain it, and saves public bodies from dealing with several requests for the same information. It should also be available to Parliament as a key part of the democratic scrutiny of public bodies. All executive quangos are already required to publish an annual report and accounts in a single document. Although there is central guidance on what it should contain, there appears to be considerable variety in the type of information provided and to what level of detail.

We recommend that executive NDPBs, supported by their sponsor departments, should:

> **a. develop their own codes of openness, building on the government code and developing good practice on the lines recommended in this report;**
>
> **b. ensure that the public are aware of the provisions of their codes;**

Sponsor departments should:

> **c. encourage executive bodies to follow best practice and improve consistency between similar bodies by working to bring the standards of all up to those of the best;**

The Cabinet Office should:

> **d. produce and periodically update guidance on good practice in openness for executive NDPBs and NHS bodies.**

Training & Induction

124.   While people recruited from outside the public sector to run public bodies can bring with them fresh ideas and valuable skills, they may not have an immediate understanding of public sector practices and why such importance is attached to the use of proper procedures when dealing with public money. Appropriate training may be needed, particularly at the induction stage.

125.   The extent to which induction training is undertaken varies greatly between different quangos. The NHS has a reasonably good record, partly reflecting the work of the National Association of Health Authorities and Trusts (NAHAT) which has established a Centre for NHS Board Development. One of the modules in their programme covers issues of corporate governance, including the NHS codes of conduct and accountability and

A *Standard of Best Practice for Openness in Executive NDPBs & NHS Bodies*

Access to information

- Adoption of a specific code on access to information incorporating the Government's code, and building on it where possible.

- Clear and published procedures for implementing the code, including:

    - well defined criteria for information that will be withheld, which should be cited whenever a request for information is refused;

    - standards for speed of response to enquiries (eg. information to be provided normally within 21 days or correspondent informed of likely date);

    - an appeal mechanism, within the organisation initially and then either to the Ombudsman, or (where the body does not come under the Ombudsman's jurisdiction) to another independent person appointed for the purpose;

    - a policy on charging for information provided (with requests requiring only a reasonable amount of work incurring no charge).

Meetings

- Opening meetings to the public or making minutes of meetings (and main committees) available for public inspection or describing key discussions and decisions in newsletters etc after each meeting. Some items may be deemed confidential, but the criteria for doing so should be published.

- A well publicised Annual General Meeting open to public and media, allowing an opportunity to question the board members on the performance and activities of the body.

- Other opportunities taken to involve and inform the public and organisation with a major interest, through consumer groups or user forums; or public meetings on major issues.

Publications

- Annual Report & Accounts, including information on the role & remit of the body, long term plans or strategy; membership of the board, performance against key targets; targets for the forthcoming year; their commitment & approach to open government; and where further information can be obtained (including how to inspect the register of board members interests and how to pursue complaints).

- Other important information to be routinely published. Depending on the body this might include key statistics; the results of consultation exercises; details of key procedures (eg criteria for allocating public funds); reports of regulatory investigations etc.

- All publications should be made as widely available as possible, such as through public libraries, and all annual reports & accounts should be deposited in the Parliamentary libraries.

establishing the values of the organisation. Over 80% of NHS trust members have received induction training, compared with around a half of Further Education Corporation members and a third of board members of Urban Development Corporations.

We recommend that new board members should on appointment make a commitment to undertake induction training which should include awareness of public sector values, and standards of probity and accountability.

126.   NAHAT also proposed in their evidence to us that training should start before candidates are selected, by holding briefing sessions for potential candidates to ensure that they are well aware of the roles they would be asked to assume. We commend this approach to departments wherever sufficient numbers are involved to make it a viable option.

Annex 1

a) : Major Executive Non-Departmental Public bodies—1993/94

Non-Departmental Public body	Department	Expenditure in £ million funded by Government	Number of Appointments
Higher Education Funding Council	Education	2,793	15
Further Education Funding Council	Education	2,683	14
Housing Corporation	Environment	1,795	13
6 Research Councils	Cabinet Office	1,150	93
Legal Aid Board	Lord Chancellor's Office	1,021	14
5 Education and Library Boards	Northern Ireland Office	938	181
Police Authority for Northern Ireland	Northern Ireland Office	600	20
Scottish Higher Education Funding Council	Scottish Office	415	13
Scottish Enterprise	Scottish Office	379	11
12 Urban Development Corporations	Environment	353	133
Scottish Homes	Scottish Office	320	9
British Council	Foreign Office	266¶	4¶
Criminal Injuries Compensation Authority	Home Office	181	0*
Higher Education Funding Council for Wales	Welsh Office	179	11
Housing for Wales	Welsh Office	160	7
Northern Ireland Housing Executive	Northern Ireland Office	159	10
English National Board for Nursing, Midwifery and Health Visiting	Health	146	10
Further Education Funding Council for Wales	Welsh Office	143	12
Scottish Legal Aid Board	Scottish Office	126	15
English Heritage	National Heritage	100	14
Total : 40 (12.3%)		**13,907** (92.2%)	**599†** (15.5%)
Other Executive Bodies : 285 (87.7%)		**1,173** (7.8%)	**3,278‡** (84.5%)
Overall total : 325		**15,080**	**3,850**

Source: Public Bodies 1994

*   New body.

†   Excludes 3 vacancies.

‡   Excludes 30 vacancies.

¶   British Council's own figures are £243m; 2

Annex 1 (continued)

b) : Major NHS bodies—1993/94

NHS body	Department	Expenditure in £ million funded by Government	Number of Appointments
8 Regional Health Authorities	Health		46
108 District Health Authorities	Health		619
89 Family Health Services Authorities	Health	18,482	862
420 NHS Trusts	Health		2,436
8 Special Health Authorities for London Postgraduate Teaching Hospitals	Health	325*	11
Special Hospital Services Authority	Health	118	5
4 Health & Social Services Boards	Northern Ireland Office	1,251	26
13 Health & Social Services Trusts	Northern Ireland Office		74
15 Health Boards	Scottish Office	3,655	102
39 NHS Trusts	Scottish Office		232
9 District Health Authorities	Welsh Office		33
8 Family Health Service Authorities	Welsh Office	1,207	79
24 NHS Trusts	Welsh Office		130
Total : 746 *(96.8%)*		**25,038** *(98.5%)*	**4,655†** *(92.8%)*
Other Executive Bodies : 24 *(3.2%)*		**359** *(1.5%)*	**360‡** *(7.2%)*
Overall total : 770		**25,398**	**5,015**

Source: Public Bodies 1994

*   1992/3 figures

†   Excludes 166 vacancies.

‡   Excludes 20 vacancies.

Annex 2

Our comments on the Review of Guidance on Public Appointments, January 1995 (The PAU Review)

PAU Review Recommendations	Our comments
The aims of an effective public appointments process should be endorsed by Ministers and set out in central & departmental guidance.	*Agree. These aims should include an explicit statement of the principle of selection on merit; and emphasise the need to maintain achieving a balance of different skills & experience on each board.* *The same principles should apply to NHS bodies as well as NDPBs (this applies to all the recommendations).*

Best practice in making appointments including agreed, clear and documented details of:
  - *the job to be done;*
  - *the qualities & experience sought;*
  - *the length of the appointment;*
  - *termination/reappointment procedures;*
  - *remuneration if any;*
  - *performance monitoring;*
  - *the code of conduct required;*
  - *induction & training required.*
All mandatory on departments subject to test of proportionality.
	Agree.
	
	Need to ensure that proportionality is not applied too widely. Agree with report that where best practice steps not followed the reasons should be recorded ie. "burden of proof" lies with those suggesting less rigour.
	
	Also proportionality should be applied primarily according to the power & influence of the body, particularly the amount of public funding it receives, rather than in relation to the remuneration or hours of the appointee.
	
	It should be mandatory on departments to make this information available to candidates and anyone else who wishes to see it, from the beginning of the appointments process.

More open advertising, easier access to information, ensuring propriety and proper disclosure of interests	*Agree (see comments below)*
Departments should consider systematically the use of advertising, search consultants and databases (with a presumption in favour of advertising)	*Agree.*
Reasons for decisions by Ministers and officials should be recorded and can, where appropriate be disclosed.	*Agree. This will provide a basis for the Public Appointments Commissioner's monitoring & auditing of Departments procedures.*

Annex 2 (continued)

PAU Review Recommendations	Our comments
Departments should ensure that, for each public body, the identity of appointees is available on demand to anyone who wishes to know. Sponsor departments should hold copies of this information centrally and know where to direct enquiries about particular bodies. In addition, most appointments of whatever kind should be publicly announced either to the local, regional or national press.	*Agree. Information should be available both from the quango itself and from the sponsor department. Public announcement of all appointments—either individually or in regular batches—should be mandatory.* *Departments should also be required to report to Parliament annually on the appointments made to executive NDPBs & NHS bodies, including any significant changes in procedures.*
Further work should be put in hand to establish the feasibility and cost of providing access, through a database linked to the Internet system, of the essential details of individual NDPBs and appointees.	*Agree.*
Party political affiliation should not normally be relevant to appointments decisions and, exceptionally, where it is, such selection considerations should be made explicit.	*Agree.*
Awaiting Nolan Committee's views on the disclosure of political office-holding	*See paras 64–69*
Discontinue process of consulting Chief Whip (except in circumstances of political sensitivity as set out in QPM). Whips of all parties to be consulted as part of regular search for names to add to database of potential candidates.	*Agree.*
Screening processes should be carefully examined by departments. For short-listed candidates written references should normally be taken up and interviews undertaken.	*It should also be mandatory for the screening process to include an independent element, through broad advisory committees or, where numbers justify, specific sifting panels. This would build on the new NHS procedures.*
Arrangements should be put in place to ensure that candidates match standards of probity required and there are no problems with conflicts of interest, including those arising from multiple appointments.	*Agree. And it is also important to ensure that no individual is appointed to more public offices than can be undertaken thoroughly and conscientiously.*

Annex 2 (continued)

PAU Review Recommendations	Our comments
Departments should sustain vigorously the programmes to promote and deliver equal opportunity principles.	*Agree. This is an integral part of promoting diversity and balance on NDPB and NHS boards.*
Departments should regularly benchmark their processes against the best in the Civil Service, and the PAU should facilitate this. Departmental processes should be reviewed as part of internal audit cycles, normally every 5 years.	*Benchmarking & promulgating good practice will be a key role of the Public Appointments Commissioner, supported by an administrative arm based on the PAU. This might include learning from appointments processes outside the Civil Service too.* *Internal audit might have a role, but an external discipline is also required. Auditing departmental systems should be undertaken on a sample basis by the Public Appointments Commissioner.*
The central guidance should be reviewed to take account of Ministers' views on the PAU Review and recommendation by the Nolan Committee.	*We welcome this. The Public Appointments Commissioner should undertake the review.*

Annex 3

Our comments on the proposed arrangements for NHS Appointments from 1 April 1995

NHS Proposals	Our comments
Aim of achieving the widest range of candidates, through advertising of vacancies (individual & composite), search agencies & databases, self-nomination, information days/ open access seminars, and standardised leaflets plus local information where required.	Agree. We also agree that "proportionality" should apply, with the reasons for not undertaking any of these approaches being clearly documented and capable of audit or review by the Public Appointments Commissioner.
Equal opportunities policy. Appointments on merit, but desirable that boards reflect population balance nationally & locally.	Agree.
Sifting should be conducted by a panel consisting of at least three local chairmen or non-executives (but not from the same board). The panel may include an independent member, eg. a member of a local Community Health Council, JP, local employer or voluntary agency.	It should be mandatory for at least one member of each panel to be independent (in keeping with our guideline of one-third independent members). Local authorities are other possible sources of independent members. The guidance does not mention taking up references or conducting interviews. This should be mandatory, except where an existing board member with a clear track record is clearly the best candidate from the initial sift.
Sifting of candidates against agreed criteria. The standard national job descriptions will form the basis of the selection criteria in every case.	Agree. And the criteria should be available to potential candidates and the public.
Where a nominee for appointment as chairman was previously an NHS non-executive with a track record, formal sifting may not be necessary.	Re-appointments should not be automatic. The performance of the post-holder should be reviewed. A balance should be struck between maintaining continuity on boards and recruiting new members to inject fresh ideas.
Health authority and trust board chairmen should give Regional Policy Board Members (RPBMs) an assessment of the performance of all non-executive directors who are to be considered for re-appointment. RPBMs will take account of this in recommendations to Ministers.	As set out in the PAU Review of NDPB appointments, there should be clear and documented details of the way in which the performance of non-executives, chairmen and RPBMs is to be monitored.

Annex 3 (continued)

NHS Proposals	Our comments
Recommendations to Ministers on the appointment of chairmen must include at least one alternative credible candidate. Where names are submitted for an entire board, Ministers should have a choice of names but not necessarily an alternative for each post.	Chairs should be subject to approval by a sifting panel, as for other non-executives.
RPBMs should consult all local MPs on candidates intended for nomination to Ministers as chairmen.	There may be a case for consulting more widely eg. with chairmen of Community Health Councils or leaders of local authorities
Regional offices should maintain a database of persons appointed.	Agree. In accordance with the PAU Review, the information should also be held centrally and be available to the public.
The same information should be held on those identified by the sifting panels as suitable for appointment but waiting a vacancy.	Agree. This information should not be available to the public.
RPBMs should be responsible to Ministers for the integrity and effectiveness of the appointments process, supported by the NHS Executive who will need to make appropriate resources available.	Agree, but there should also be external monitoring. NHS appointments should fall within the remit of the new Public Appointments Commissioner.
Regional offices should ensure, with support from the NHS Executive, that appropriate training for non-executive directors is provided at both local and national level.	Agree. The training, particularly at induction stage, should cover the NHS codes of conduct & accountability, and other issues of propriety.

Appendix 1

Standards in Public Life: Twentieth century cases of misconduct and current public opinion*

It seems to me that these kind of troubles about malpractices...or mistrust of Ministers and Parliament rather go in cycles. From about 1860 to 1895 there was very little trouble of that sort, but from 1895 onwards there was a lot. ... From 1895 to 1930 was a period when a lot of financial scandals were going on, but it was succeeded by a period of relative quiescence...But something has happened more recently, and I think it may be partly connected...with a sort of get rich quick mentality which very much prevailed in the Edwardian era, and I think has been prevailing quite a lot in the last 20 years.

Lord Blake

The Turn of the Century

1. Between the turn of the century and the outbreak of the First World War the Marconi scandal of 1911–13 stands out. Two Government Ministers (one of them the Chancellor of the Exchequer, David Lloyd George) bought shares in the American Marconi company before they went on sale to the general public but after the British Government, as they knew, had signed a large and lucrative contract with the separate British Marconi company. The Government Chief Whip also bought shares on behalf of the Liberal party. The American Marconi shares, after going on sale, doubled in value.

2. The Ministers at first attempted to conceal what they had done, then, when they were found out, claimed that, despite appearances, they had not been guilty of any wrongdoing. They suffered no adverse political consequences (apart from embarrassment). One went on to become Prime Minister, the other Lord Chief Justice and Viceroy of India. The House of Commons select committee set up to investigate the affair divided along party lines in the Ministers' favour, as did the House itself. Neither major newspapers nor (perhaps as a consequence) the general public took much interest in the affair.

Between the Wars

3. A feeling that standards in public life had declined appears to have been fairly widespread in the period immediately following the First World War. Doubts were

---

* More information relating to this section will be found in two books: Alan Doig, Corruption and Misconduct in Contemporary British Politics (Penguin 1984); and G R Searle, Corruption in British Politics, 1985–1930 (OUP 1987).

expressed about the awarding of wartime contracts, and the Coalition Government's sale of honours to augment party funds attracted increasing opprobrium. Ministers repeatedly misled Parliament, denying that honours were for sale; but King George V was incensed, describing the offer of a peerage to a businessman recently convicted of fraud as 'little less than an insult to the Crown and the House of Lords'.

4.   In 1922, the Government conceded that something was wrong and established a Royal Commission on Honours. Its report, which was accepted, recommended that political candidates for honours should be vetted by three privy councillors, none of whom should be a member of the government of the day. This system is still in place.

5.   The fall of Lloyd George and the Coalition led to a conscious effort in the following decades both to raise standards and rigorously to enforce those already in existence. Stanley Baldwin deliberately contrasted his sobriety with the flamboyance of Lloyd George. Scandals involving financial abuse or the abuse of power, although not unknown in the late 1920s, 1930s and 1940s, were remarkably few.

The Post-War Period

6.   The one Minister who fell foul of the new, more stringent standards immediately after the Second World War was a junior Board of Trade Minister, John Belcher. Belcher, who was in a position to influence the issuing of government licences and permits (against the backdrop of tight postwar controls), became friendly with a number of businessmen from whom he accepted gifts. In return, Belcher was said to have given improper official favours. Prime Minister Attlee set up a Tribunal of Inquiry under Mr Justice Lynskey to investigate. The Tribunal concluded that Belcher (though no other Ministers and officials) had behaved improperly, and Belcher at once resigned his Ministerial office (and subsequently his seat in the House of Commons).

The Fifties and Sixties

7.   Another two decades passed before similar charges were laid against anyone else in a position of major responsibility. The well-publicised scandals of the late 1950s and early 1960s all involved sexual rather than financial or political impropriety, though in some cases issues of national security were also raised.

The Seventies

8.   Financial impropriety on a major scale was however revealed in the early 1970s. The architect John Poulson befriended civil servants, local councillors, local council officials, nationalised industry and NHS employees, and Members of Parliament, paid them varying amounts in cash and kind and then used their influence to secure contracts.

9.   As a result of their involvement with Poulson, senior officials in central and local government, as well as prominent local politicians, were imprisoned, as was Poulson

himself. The then Home Secretary, Reginald Maudling, and two other MPs were criticised by a House of Commons Select Committee. Two inquiries followed: a committee under Lord Redcliffe-Maud to enquire into problems of conflict of interest in local government; and a Royal Commission into Standards of Conduct in Public Life (the Salmon Commission). Substantial new rules were put in place for the conduct of local government.

The Present Day

10. Claims that the highest public standards were not being adhered to were made on occasion during the 1980s; but in the early 1990s there was a spate of such accusations. Taken singly, none of the allegations was in the same league as the Marconi or Poulson scandals—or even the Belcher affair. Taken together, they seemed to many people to create a pervasive atmosphere of 'sleaze', in which sexual, financial and governmental misconduct were indifferently linked.

11. The allegations of sexual misbehaviour made against public figures, followed in most cases by resignation, have become almost too numerous to remember. They have been, for the most part, essentially private rather than public in character, and the performance of official duties has not been compromised. The same cannot be said of the cases that have raised questions about financial propriety. In recent years these have included payments for asking parliamentary questions and other action on behalf of clients in Parliament; the employment of ex-Ministers and former officials by firms that they have privatised or with which they had other direct dealings; alleged links between political donations and appointments; fraud and misspending in quangos, such as the Welsh Development Agency; and allegations that Ministers had accepted personal favours that created conflicts of interest with their public duties.

12. In addition to questions of financial impropriety, allegations have also been made that involve the real or alleged abuse of governmental power. In recent years allegations under this heading have included the arms to Iraq affair (the subject of a current inquiry by Sir Richard Scott), corruption and wrongdoing in local councils of all political complexions, the appointment of people to quangos on purely political grounds, and the reluctance of Ministers to resign over their mistakes. Public concern about all these matters led the Prime Minister to set up this Committee in October 1994.

Current Public Opinion

13. Public opinion polling began in Britain only in the late 1930s and, until quite recently, the number of questions asked by the polls about standards in public life has been very small. For example, the Gallup Poll asked no questions at all about Belcher and the Lynskey Tribunal, or about Poulson.

14. Indeed only the recent spate of allegations and the suggestion that they form an overall patten of 'sleaze' has provoked the polls into asking larger numbers of questions relating (however loosely in some cases) to standards in public life. The results of these recent polls are not encouraging.

15. Market and Opinion Research International (MORI) in 1983 and again in 1993 offered respondents a list of people in different occupations and asked of each: 'Would you tell me whether you generally trust them to tell the truth or not?' The results suggest that Ministers and politicians vie with journalists for being the least trusted occupational category in the country. As Table 1 shows, a majority of MORI's groups actually improved their standing between 1983 and 1993; but the standing of Ministers and politicians, already low, fell still further.

Table 1 : Public Standing of Occupational Groups

	% 'generally trusting them to tell the truth'		Change
	1983	1993	
Clergymen/Priests	85	80	–5
Doctors	82	84	+2
Teachers	79	84	+5
Judges	77	68	–9
Professors	n/a	70	-
Television news readers	63	72	+9
The police	61	63	+2
Ordinary person in the street	57	64	+7
Pollsters	n/a	52	-
Civil servants	25	37	+12
Business leaders	25	32	+7
Journalists	19	10	–9
Trade Union Officials	18	32	+14
Politicians generally	18	14	–4
Government ministers	16	11	–5

16. Like MORI, the Gallup Poll asked a question about standards of members of Parliament approximately a decade ago and repeated it more recently. Interviewers read out a list of statements about 'most members of parliament' and asked respondents whether they agreed or disagreed with each or had no opinion. Table 2, comparing 1985 with 1994, suggests that the level or public distrust of, and alienation from, MPs, already high 10 years ago, has grown substantially since.

TABLE 2 : Standards of Members of Parliament

	% agreeing, disagreeing with each statement	
	1985	*1994*
Most MPs make a lot of money by using public office improperly		
Agree	46	64
Disagree	31	22
Don't know	23	14
Most MPs have a high personal moral code		
Agree	42	28
Disagree	35	59
Don't know	23	15
Most MPs will tell lies if they feel the truth will hurt them politically		
Agree	79	87
Disagree	12	8
Don't know	9	5
Most MPs care more about special interests than they care about people like you		
Agree	67	77
Disagree	19	12
Don't know	14	11

17. A Gallup survey in November 1994 was devoted largely to questions of standard in public life and was published in the Daily Telegraph under the (accurate) headline, 'voters pass severe judgement on politicians' moral standards. Sixty-seven per cent of those polled felt that "the ethical and moral standards of British politicians have been declining in recent years". The poll also revealed the high standards which the public expected of their members of Parliament.

TABLE 3 : What an MP should not accept

	% feeling it was right/not right to accept	
	Right	**Not Right**
Payment for asking questions in Parliament	2	95
A free holiday abroad	6	92
Money or gifts in connection with Parliamentary duties	7	89
Payment for giving advice about Parliamentary matters	9	85
Free tickets to Wimbledon and other major sporting events	25	69
Free lunch at restaurant	48	47
Bottles of wine or whisky at Christmas	51	45

Appendix 2

Glossary of initials used in this Report

C&AG	Comptroller and Auditor General
CIPFA	Chartered Institute of Public Finance and Accountancy
CSMC	Civil Service Management Code
INLOGOV	Institute of Local Government, at Birmingham University
MORI	Market and Opinion Research International
MP	Member of Parliament
NAHAT	National Association of Health Authorities and Trusts
NAO	National Audit Office
NDPB	Non-Departmental Public Body
NHS	National Health Service
OPSS	Office of Public Service and Science
PAU	Public Appointments Unit (at present part of the Office of Public Service and Science)
PCA	Parliamentary Commissioner for Administration—the Central Government Ombudsman
PQ	Parliamentary Question
QPM	Questions of Procedure for Ministers
Quango	Quasi-Autonomous Non-Governmental Organisation
RHA	Regional Health Authority
RPBM	Regional Policy Board Member (of the NHS)
TCSC	Treasury and Civil Service Select Committee

recycled
paper

Printed in the United Kingdom for HMSO
Dd 5064148.   5/95   C60.   51–8434.   48003.